THE CRITICS DEBATE

General Editor: Michael Scott

Y0-BQI-064

The Critics Debate
General Editor: Michael Scott

MEASURE FOR MEASURE

T.F. Wharton

HUMANITIES PRESS INTERNATIONAL, INC.
Atlantic Highlands, NJ

First published 1989 by
HUMANITIES PRESS INTERNATIONAL, INC.,
Atlantic Highlands, NJ 07716

©T.F. Wharton, 1989

Library of Congress Cataloging-in-Publication Data
Wharton, T.F.
  Measure for measure.
  (The Critics debate)
  Bibliography: p.
  Includes index.
  1. Shakespeare, William, 1564–1616.   Measure for
  measure. I. Title. II. Series.
PR2824.W44   1989   822.3′3   88–26673
ISBN 0–391–03625–4
ISBN 0–391–03626–2 (Pbk)

Printed in Hong Kong

Contents

To my daughter
Rebecca

General Editor's Preface

OVER THE last few years the practice of literary criticism has become hotly debated. Methods developed earlier in the century and before have been attacked and the word "crisis" has been drawn upon to describe the present condition of English Studies. That such a debate is taking place is a sign of the subject discipline's health. Some would hold that the situation necessitates a radical alternative approach which naturally implies a "crisis situation". Others would respond that to employ such terms is to precipitate or construct a false position. The debate continues but it is not the first. "New Criticism" acquired its title because it attempted something fresh, calling into question certain practices of the past. Yet the practices it attacked were not entirely lost or negated by the new critics. One factor becomes clear: English Studies is a pluralistic discipline.

What are students, coming to advanced work in English for the first time, to make of all this debate and controversy? They are in danger of being overwhelmed by the cross-currents of critical approaches as they take up their study of literature. The purpose of this series is to help delineate various critical approaches to specific literary texts. Its authors are from a variety of critical schools and have approached their task in a flexible manner. Their aim is to help the reader come to terms with the variety of criticism and to introduce him or her to further reading on the subject and to a fuller evaluation of a particular text by illustrating the way it has been approached in a number of contexts. In the first part of the book a critical survey is given of some of the major ways the text has been appraised. This is done sometimes in a thematic manner, sometimes according to various "schools" or "approaches". In the second part the authors provide their own appraisals of the text from their stated critical standpoint, allowing the reader the knowledge of their own particular approaches from which their views may in turn be evaluated. The series therein hopes to introduce and to elucidate criticism of authors and texts being studied and to encourage participation as the critics debate.

Michael Scott

Introduction

Measure for Measure is currently Shakespeare's most popular play. This is a curious fact, since no writer has ever claimed that it is in the same league dramatically as the great tragedies. On the contrary, its imperfections are obvious, and many consider it to be at best an interesting artistic failure. Yet, any given year will yield a flood of productions of the play. In one amazing year – 1981 – even apart from performances in London and the Edinburgh Festival, the play was given major productions in three different American Shakespeare Festivals, and in Switzerland, Hungary, Belgium, and China. No doubt it was also performed by amateur drama groups from Durham to Darwin. In scholarship, too, the play is hugely popular. A printout of the articles written on the play over the last seven years lists 150 entries. This torrent of industry inspired by the play, and unexplainable in terms of its pure literary merit, can only be accounted for by supposing that in some ways it strikes a chord which vibrates to our own times. It is, for a start, a play of much darkness and uncertainty, of political corruption, spying, and sexual decadence. As Michael Scott, general editor of this series says, 'it is a rich play for an uneasy decade' (1982). Its contemporary appeal has been emphasised by the ease with which the play can be done in modern dress, up to and including 'punk'.

The familiarity is far from comfortable, however. This is a play which consistently disturbs and puzzles us, and leaves us unsure of our bearings. To compare it with the great tragedies Shakespeare wrote within a year or so of it is instructive. Whatever debate the tragedies provoke, nobody would ever dream of asking whether it was right or wrong for Othello to kill his innocent wife, or whether *Macbeth* is really a tragedy. These things are self-evident. Yet, it is exactly such basic certainties which *Measure for Measure* denies us.

We are not sure, for a start, of the ethical issues. Our

uncertainty begins with the 'justice' of a law which sentences an engaged man to death for sleeping with his fiancée; or with the 'virtue' of the upright judge who carries out the law with such enthusiasm; or with the 'goodness' of the Duke who puts such a judge in absolute power. There is 'poetic justice', of course, when that judge himself 'falls', but we must then ponder the morality of the condemned man's sister's decision to let him die, rather than sacrifice her chastity (a problem complicated by her status as a novice nun). We then have to work out the ethics of the Duke's rescue of the condemned man by arranging the judge's fornication with his abandoned fiancée. In other words, every major figure in the play is involved in moral doubt or contradiction. They are not even easy to like.

Equally, we are not sure that this is a comedy, or indeed what kind of play it is. The major issue here is the combination of often uncomfortable material with a traditional comic ending. Many have found that combination unworkable. The most popular name-category for *Measure for Measure* is 'Problem Play', a title which E.M.W. Tillyard compares with the idea of a 'problem child', a kind of delinquent drama which nobody quite knows what to do with (1951).

*

The aim of Part One of this present book will be to explain and summarise the main responses which have emerged to these and other problems posed by the play. The organisation will follow a basic three-part division, following the three main strands of comment I can distinguish. I shall review issues of dramatic genre or type; matters of context and essential background material; and matters of theme, which necessarily includes issues of ethics and of character.

The first – genre – will look at what kind of play *Measure for Measure* is, according to the critics: comedy, tragi-comedy, Problem Play, or whatever. If the term 'Problem Play' has any precise meaning, it either means that the play contains very strong moral problems, or that its type is highly uncertain. As to the last, the play is supposed to be a comedy, but for almost half its length reads nothing like one. On the contrary, the beginning leads us to believe that the principal figures – Angelo and Isabella especially – are likely, with their colliding wills, their over-zealous virtues, to drive the play towards tragic ends, not comic ones. *Measure for Measure*, in short, promises to be a tragedy. Yet, the conflicts are all abruptly headed off, and the characters denied the freedom to destroy themselves. As soon as the Duke begins to control the action, he robs the characters of the consequences, however disastrous, of their decisions. Even if the play does this in the best of causes, the change of direction has vexed many. Philip Edwards speaks of our being 'cheated' by the transformation (1968). It is accordingly the 'problem' of mixed dramatic type which will occupy most space in the section on genre. The discussion will also, however, include material on the play's sources and dramatic devices ('bed-trick', 'disguised Duke', etc.). These help us to read Shakespeare's mind. By discovering where his material came from, and how he changed it, we can see something of the directions he thought he was going in. This has considerable bearing on the issue of dramatic type.

The second main section of Part One will deal with essential context and background. The usefulness of this is that by, as it were, asking Shakespeare's contemporaries what they thought, for instance, of militant virgins or manipulative rulers, we can seek guidance on how to respond to characters in the play who leave our natural and unaided sympathies confused or in conflict. This section will accordingly review the scholarly evidence on exactly these things, especially 'manipulative rulers'. England's new king, James I, at whose court *Measure for Measure* was performed within a year of his accession, had pronounced views on the rights, privileges, and duties of kings. Shakespeare's portrait of 'Vincentio' may turn out to be less the picture of a fictional Viennese Duke than of his own newly-crowned monarch. Even if it is not, a study of political theory in Shakespeare's day sheds valuable light on how we should react to the apparently meddlesome ruler, Vincentio.

Again, since part of the ethical problems posed by the play concern sex and marriage, this section will look at Elizabethan and Jacobean marital law, and its apparent view that a betrothal was automatically converted into marriage by the sex-act.

The last main division of critical opinion handled in Part One of the book will be thematic. Broadly speaking, those who handle issues of theme are the ones most anxious to find an optimistic message in a disturbing play. Accordingly, this section will assemble and summarise evidence of the play's interest in Mercy and Justice. The two are by no means always on the same side. In *Measure for Measure*, they seem antagonistic. For some critics, this antagonism is the principal interest that the play holds, and they argue that Shakespeare makes Mercy triumph over mere Justice, in ways which echo his society's concern that there should be specific courts of appeal (the courts of 'equity') to correct legal injustices. Some of these theorists have pushed the idea of 'Mercy' one step further. For them, the play is specifically Christian in content, a kind of allegory or mirror of God's salvation of man. In this interpretation, the Duke becomes a type of 'power divine'; his subjects represent fallen mankind; and his rescue of Claudio, Angelo, and Isabella parallels divine redemption; especially since it involves the replacement of the Old Law of rigorous 'Justice', with the New Law of 'Mercy'.

However, there is no theory about the play which has aroused more hostility from rival critics, who contrast this redemptive moral with some of the less savory aspects of the play. For these critics, both the plot and the characters fall far short of the moral they are meant to uphold. For instance, the sometimes absurd plot-contrivances of the second half – the 'bed-trick' or the exchange of heads – or the very imperfect Duke who engineers them (and whom we are meant to accept as 'God'): all these things seem either to prove that no such Christian theme was ever intended, or that, if it was intended, Shakespeare forced it on the wrong material, and only by an intolerable deal of manipulation of plot and character. Again, this section of Part One will examine in some detail all that has been alleged against the Christian theme, the characters and the plot. Most recently the attack has centred on the Duke, and this section will particularly feature the lively feminist criticism which has lately been directed against him.

In Part Two, I offer my own interpretation of the play, which also centres on the Duke. I view him neither as divine power nor bungler, but as a moral experimenter, using his dukedom as a laboratory in which to discover and exploit the breaking-points of his subjects, both 'virtuous' and vicious. His assumptions about human nature are sceptical: his motives are curiosity and power.

Throughout Part One, I shall make a determined effort to combine comment on the theoretical issues with some attention to how the play has recently been handled in the theatre. It was written, after all, for the stage; actors and directors as much as literary critics are involved in interpreting the play; and their responses often provide potent guides to our own.

Part One: Survey

I Form, genesis, genre

It was Frederick Boas who more than eighty years ago first offered the description of *Measure for Measure*, along with three other Shakespeare works, as a 'Problem Play'. His definition of the term is teasingly vague, but he mentions both the complexity of moral problems which these plays contain, and the impression that they seem to be neither truly comic nor tragic.

Clearly, Boas's bafflement as to what to call the play must be based on a clear sense of what a Shakespeare comedy or tragedy is usually like, and it is here that the whole issue of the play's dramatic type should properly open. Actually, since the play is clearly closer to comedy than to tragedy on even the most primitive of definitions, we should begin with at least some tentative definitions of the norms of the comic form.

Laughter is possibly its least significant component. Shakespeare himself left us no thoughts on this subject, but his contemporaries often actively decried laughter in comedy. The satirist Ben Jonson flatly called it a 'fault'. The writer of romantic comedy, John Lyly, preferred 'soft smiling' to 'loud laughing'. Sir Philip Sidney, in his work of literary theory, *An Apology for Poetry* (by which he meant all creative writing) contrasted the mere 'scornful tickling' of laughter with 'delight', a quality he regards as intrinsic to comedy; bred by our delight in beauty, happiness, or sudden good fortune. Later writers on comic theory have often agreed that there are more solid satisfactions in comedy than a few laughs. For Freud it was the vicarious triumph of the ego over adversity. For Meredith it was the admission-ticket to a benevolent world. For C.L. Barber, writing specifically on Shakespeare, it was a festive celebration of primitive energy.

The common impression here is of comedy's power to involve us in its predominantly happy events, and make us identify with and rejoice in the triumphs of its main characters. From Sidney onwards, those triumphs are defined in terms of obstacles overcome.

The most influential writer on comic form in recent times has been Northrop Frye. In his most informative book on the subject, he writes of Shakespearean comedy's three-part structure: the initial obstruction to the comic drive (often an irrational law); a central period of confusion and mistaken identity; and the final triumph over obstacles. Since Shakespeare's comic heroes and heroines are invariably in love, the obstacles they encounter are obstacles to their union; the arena of confusion is often a forest or 'green world' in which we are aware of strong reproductive rhythms; and the final triumph consists of their unimpeded marriage (1965).

Measure for Measure has strong affinities with this pattern. Clearly, at the beginning of the play, there is an irrational law which operates against a pair of lovers (one of whom, Juliet, incidentally bears a name highly expressive of virtuous love). Certainly, there is a central period of disguise and of great confusion of events. Clearly, too, the ending overturns the irrational law, and the play ends with marriages. There is a strong outbreak of what Anne Barton calls 'the pairing-off disease' (1974), with Angelo marrying Mariana, Claudio united with Juliet, the Duke proposing to Isabella, and Lucio marrying his whore. True, there is no 'green world', but Shakespeare's *Twelfth Night* and *Much Ado About Nothing* are equally devoid of one, and are still unquestionably 'comedies'. Apart from this, the play seems to fit almost perfectly to Frye's theory. In the formal sense it is clearly a comedy, to the extent that one might even wonder what all the fuss is about, concerning the play's type. Furthermore, even if we concede that laughter is not actually necessary in a comedy, *Measure for Measure* contains plenty of it. As Arthur Kirsch points out, the play has an unusually well-developed comic low-life sector, at least as extensive as that of *Twelfth Night* (1975); and W.W. Lawrence rightly says that, however base these characters' motives and sentiments, they still remain 'live men, pleasing to Shakespeare' (1931).

Tone

Certainly, some productions have chosen to emphasise the play's genuine humorous possibilities. The Joe Papp production in New York's Central Park in 1985 clearly surrendered the play to this dimension, with the low-life scenes in particular milked for comedy, but even the Duke being played as a minor Wodehouse silly-ass figure, and costumes and set suggesting a kind of toy-town Ruritania. The 1979 Stratford production likewise treated the Duke lightly, casting him in the mould of a cricketing cleric, with an impish, hearty manner. Most determinedly cheery of all was the decision of the National Theatre in 1981 to set the play in the West Indies, with an all-black cast. For the 'Vienna' of this production it was carnival time, and Isabella responded to the Duke's wedding proposal by dashing up the steps to give him a hearty hug.

Yet, other productions have sensed and promoted a very different tone in the play, and such dark-toned productions easily outnumber the sunnier interpretations. Michael Scott (1982) notes the way directors seem drawn to claustrophobic sets for the play. Cubes and boxes predominate, suggesting a sense of imprisonment. Many productions use specific barred-prison motifs, echoing some recent writings on the play – for instance P.S. Spinrad's – which see the play as containing many prison-like enclosures: walled convent, moated grange, double-locked garden, and of course the prison itself (1984).

Again, some productions go much further. The 1985 Stratford Ontario production by Michael Bogdanov made a wholesale attempt to incorporate as many disturbing effects and rever-berations from our own times as he could devise; spilling out well beyond the play in doing so. There was a half-hour cabaret as unofficial prologue, with a pair of transvestites in chains and leather, and a tough stripper circulating through the fascinated and appalled audience. The 'club' was subsequently raided, and images of riot police, strobe lights, and a barrage of helicopter sound returned to haunt the ending. In a production of much unfocused groping, kissing and caressing, it was a far from festive world, but rather a Vienna of profound decadence which here emerged. While such a production has no authoritative claim to represent the 'truth' about *Measure for Measure*, the play's receptiveness to such images of violence and sexuality is an eloquent proof that this can be no simple 'comedy'. In fact, it may establish that any reading which refuses to acknowledge its disturbing elements is blinding itself to something fundamental in the play.

Sexuality

Bogdanov's production does no more than realise on stage what many have perceived on the page: that the play is to an extraordinary extent filled with the idea of sexuality. Not a single critic sees this as a sign of the play's health. As to the cause, there are those who, like David Holbrook, simply believe that Shakespeare himself 'had problems with sexuality' (1986), those who, like Richard Wheeler, detect a sex-obsession only in the plays from 1600 onwards (1981), or those who, like Harriet Hawkins, see a lack of moral consensus in the age as a whole (1978). Whatever the reason, though, David Lloyd Stevenson neatly sums up the feelings of many when he writes that 'the insistently frank treatment accorded to sex throughout *Measure for Measure* . . . is one of its peculiar and noticeable features. *Measure for Measure*, unlike Shakespeare's romantic comedies or his love-game comedies, involves us directly and almost continually with, and in comment on, the act of sex' (1966). As to the 'comment on' sex, many have noticed the sheer quantity of obscene puns: recent work has added words hitherto thought to be innocent, like 'sickles', 'tested', 'fault', or 'stewed prunes', to the list. As to the continual involvement with sex, psychological studies, very notably those of Hans Sachs on Angelo (1970), and of Carolyn Brown on the 'erotic flagellation' obsessions of all three of the major characters (1986), confirm that even the play's 'virtuous' figures define themselves in relation to sex, and that they finally betray as strong a sexuality – perverted into repression, sadism and masochism – as any of the low-life figures.

   This makes *Measure for Measure* a very different play from those earlier ones which were so unproblematically 'comedies'. Sex was indeed widely mentioned in those plays. There is no shortage of broad bawdy from *Love's Labours Lost* onwards. Yet the topic stopped right there, at the level of words. Even the cynic, Touchstone, somewhat against his will, does not anticipate his wedding night; and, despite, say, Don John's evil and absurd accusations in *Much Ado About Nothing*, there is not the remotest prospect of any major figure succumbing to temptation. Yet, in *Measure for Measure*, Claudio, Juliet, Angelo, Mariana, Lucio and his 'lady', and the entire low-life cast are sexually active outside or on the periphery of marriage. Also, as Mary Lascelles astutely remarks in her still-useful book, this is an oddly 'unfamilied' world, uninhabited by parents, and with much distance between brothers and sisters or even engaged couples; so that this sexual world also lacks a stabilising sense of normal bearings (1953).

Sources

The main sources for Shakespeare's story are Italian: a novella and a play by Geraldi Cinthio (1565 and 1583 respectively), as transmitted through intermediary English sources, a novella and a play by George Whetstone (1582 and 1578 respectively). As Leo Salingar says of the four Shakespeare comedies taken from Italian sources, their 'tone is more serious than usual' (1974), and certainly, this is no light tale. Cinthio provides the basic tale of the unjust and lustful judge who offers to spare a man condemned for rape on condition that his virgin sister, who had come to plead for mercy, should sleep with him. She agrees, but is betrayed: the unjust judge sends her the decapitated body of her brother. She appeals to the emperor who forces the judge to marry her, and then orders his execution. After her marriage, the lady appeals for mercy for her husband, and the Emperor grants his life. Whetstone's version softens the brother's crime from rape to the seduction of his girlfriend whom he was now willing to marry, and also saves his life by having the jailer substitute another decapitated body. The lady, though, believes him to be dead. She buries the body, appeals to the king, is married to the judge, but is about to watch his execution, when her brother appears and saves her husband's life.

Shakespeare's version makes the brother's offence even lighter (he is already engaged to Juliet). His major change, however, is to make the sister a novice nun, who refuses the judge's offer. The idea of the substituted head and the survival of the brother is kept, but he vastly expands the role of the king or emperor:

his Duke, in his disguise as Friar, is an active agent in the story, with his device of the 'bed-trick' and so forth. Finally, it is of course the Duke, not the unjust judge who marries the sister. The unjust judge marries his rejected fiancée, who substitutes for the sister in the 'bed-trick'. Josephine Waters Bennett (1966) argues that Shakespeare's changes to the sources greatly lighten them. Yet, those changes introduce at least one acute new dilemma: the dilemma of a nun, whether to save a life or, as she sees it, save her own soul. It is a dilemma which creates a tense collision of fervent desires between herself and her would-be seducer, Angelo. In all, in both the choice and handling of his sources, Shakespeare created a situation of disquiet and conflict.

Folk-tale elements

On the other hand, Shakespeare rescues Claudio and Isabella using devices from the realm of lightweight fantasy. There is, first of all, the Viennese law itself. Shakespeare, has we have noted, makes Claudio's original offence lighter. However, this also makes the law itself much harsher. This, for Margaret Scott, puts the story firmly in the realm of 'story-book law' (1982), and therefore, as W.W. Lawrence says, 'we do not need to take this "statute" too seriously'. The Duke's own role, far more extensive than in the sources, is likewise from folk-tale. Lawrence (1931) and Mary Lascelles trace the idea of the disguised ruler, observing and correcting his subjects, as far back as the medieval stories of Haroun al Raschid or the emperor Severus. If, as Rosalind Miles has pointed out, the role can be used cruelly, its main use is invariably for 'getting at the truth' (1976). An audience encountering a disguised duke like Vincentio would therefore immediately be receiving a basically reassuring signal. Again, Lawrence and Miles stress that the device of the substituted bride, more commonly known as the 'bed-trick', whereby Mariana, Angelo's rejected fiancée, acts as sexual stand-in for the virgin Isabella, is connected with the ancient folk-tale motif of the 'clever wench'. Again, it would have been regarded as a reassuring and homely device, and had been used even by modest and admirable heroines. The reward of the substitute is invariably marriage; and recent versions of the motif had also ended in the punishment of the lustful. Both these expectations would be set up in the contemporary audience as soon as the Duke proposed the plan. Finally, Josephine Bennett points out that even a tiny detail such as the Duke denying his vulnerability to the 'dribbling dart' of Cupid has a long comic ancestry, and promises that he will become love's victim before the end of the play (1966).

Tragi-comedy

One simple way out of the perennial problems of the clash between the play's more disturbing and more comic aspects is to call it, not a comedy, but a tragi-comedy. Arthur C. Kirsch is one of the more persuasive supporters of this theory, pointing out that the Italian dramatist Guarini had recently (1601) evolved a new hybrid form of this type, imitated by Shakespeare's contemporaries Beaumont and Fletcher, which called for the arousal of feelings, but not their disturbance; the threat of death without it actually happening; many reversals of plot; and more 'frisson' than real anxiety. For Kirsch (1975), Shakespeare's play fits the description exactly. It arouses our feelings but then soothes them; it threatens Claudio with death but spares him; it manipulates the plot elaborately. Yet Kirsch's arguments had already been anticipated and largely answered ten years earlier in J.W. Lever's Introduction to his Arden edition of the play (1965). For Lever, the biggest obstacle to Shakespeare's discipleship to Guarini – quite apart from the vexed question of whether he was even aware of Guarini – lies in the highly impassioned nature of the first half of the play. Here, characters are strained to breaking, and tested on the beliefs that form the very bedrock of their existence. This is Shakespeare writing at his most powerful, where 'tensions and discords are wrought up to their highest pitch, threatening the dissolution of all human values'. Lever argues that 'conflicts and dilemmas are explored with a terrible insight beyond Guarini's limited reach: the laughter remains unrepentantly dissolute; the attractions of the comic scenes are elemental rather than modest'. With Rosalind Miles reminding us that Guarini's plays are pastoral, whereas Shakespeare's is urban, the 'Guarini' theory probably sustains more damage than it can well absorb.

Comic/tragic split

What Lever argues instead is that Shakespeare's experiment in tragi-comedy is of a different kind altogether. It consists of 'two almost mathematical halves', deliberately juxtaposed: two totally different types of play within the same pages. Certainly, this theory sits well with the common impression that the play almost splits in the middle. In his more recent book specifically on the 'Problem Plays', Northrop Frye (1983) argues that the split is so severe as to make the play a 'diptych' (a picture on two panels, side by side). As he rightly observes, the language drastically changes immediately after the last great verse-scene of conflict, in which Isabella visits Claudio in prison, tells him of Angelo's plan, then savagely rebukes him for being even momentarily tempted by the prospect of having his life saved. At this point, when the Duke steps forward to speak in prose, the entire form of the play changes: 'from here on, we are engaged in a comic action, an extremely complicated intrigue, involving a bed trick, endless disguisings, and many lies. The action is stage-managed by a disguised Duke, who takes a role that is frequent and important in Shakespeare, of a kind of deputy dramatist, arranging a dramatic action within the larger design.' Tragedy is in effect replaced by comedy.

The problem

Josephine Waters Bennett is correct of course in pointing out that, with the device of the disguised Duke mentioned in the earliest scenes, this is a play which is 'highly artificial and contrived not merely from the middle of Act III but from the beginning'. Yet his disguise does not become active until the middle of Act III. Reader after reader comments, like Harriet Hawkins, on the 'extraordinary psychological and sexual reverberations of the earlier scenes'. It takes a degree of true perversity to argue, like Bennett, that Isabella 'faces no serious problems'. Surely, Anne Barton (1974) is correct in insisting that Shakespeare, in the middle of Act III, 'suddenly imposes upon a play which has probed uncomfortably deep into the dark places of society and of the human mind, which has been essentially realistic, an ending which is that of fairytale: conventional, suspect in its very tidiness, full of psychological gaps and illogicalities'.

As Harriet Hawkins observes, the critics have always finally been split between those who claim that they can forget the near-tragic nature of the play's first half, and those who cannot. An extreme case of the latter is Philip Edwards (1968), who is finally unable to forgive the play for cutting off such interesting possibilities: 'what we really want to know is what happens to a person that decides as Isabella decides? Does she relent? Does she harden? If she relents, what do she and Angelo feel after their union? If she hardens, what happens to her?' This coincides with Harriet Hawkins' view that, in a play, the characters who push their fates to the extreme are 'our fictional surrogates for our own desire to "try the uttermost"'. Many share a sense of loss, when those uttermost possibilities vanish: J.W. Lever complains that 'the autonomy of the individual is lost, and with it his innate right to choose as between evil and good'. Jean E. Howard similarly laments that the Duke seems, in the second half, to 'draw the life out of formerly vital characters like Isabella' (1983). Robert F. Willson, reviewing the 1979 BBC performance of the play, so clearly regards the Angelo/Isabella scenes as being the heart of the play that he ignores all else (1986). Even more strikingly, the Charles Marowitz adaptation of the play was designed, as Michael Scott stresses, to discover what 'would have happened', if the romantic comedy conventions had not been imposed.

With this degree of agreement between the critics that it is indeed a realistic and tragic situation which is headed off by the Duke's intervention, there can be little doubt that, even if the play does conform to all the proper features of a regular Shakespeare comedy, the characters who inhabit that form produce the sense of something far from comic.

Rosalind Miles realises clearly that in making his heroine a woman of the church, and one most unlikely to be the centre of romantic interest, Shakespeare produces a 'highly unusual heroine'. Nor is there much alternative interest residing in the nearly-invisible Juliet or Mariana, who, for Leo Salingar, is so much closeted in her 'moated grange' that she almost combines with Isabella to produce a 'double nun motif' (1974).

As to Angelo, Josephine Bennett is alone in her insistence that he is 'essentially comic', in his exaggerated rectitude. Others indeed acknowledge that there is such a stage type as the 'comic hypocrite'. Rosalind Miles, however, refuses to acknowledge Angelo as such, and Hans Sachs (1970) believes that Shakespeare stopped well short of the possible comic device of making Angelo 'the stupid dupe who gets tripped up at every step'.

Finally, with the Duke, the feminist critic Marcia Riefer forcefully reminds us (1984) just how unusual it is for a figure of senior male authority such as Vincentio, to play any dominant part in a Shakespeare comedy. Mostly, she argues, such 'patriarchal' figures are banished or ignored, so that a younger generation may conduct their love affairs without impediment. Here, however, in *Measure for Measure*, 'patriarchal authority is moved from the periphery of the normal Shakespearean comic action right to the heart of the play'. She goes on to demonstrate that his authority is hostile to the kind of love action native to romantic comedy. The Duke may indeed provide our happy ending, and happy endings are essential to a comedy. Yet, as Richard P. Wheeler says (1981), the mere presence of even the ideal paternal heritage in such a play 'produces profound conflict'.

Furthermore, some of the typical features of the comic design which we have observed to be present in the play are actually present only in distorted form. This seems particularly true of the final marriages. There are four of them, a score matched only in *As You Like It*. However trite, they usually stand, as Bernard Beckerman says, as a kind of convenient shorthand for the implied harmony of the major couples, and of the 'acts that lead up to a marriage' (1985). Yet, as Wheeler says, none of this play's marriages 'completes a relationship that has held a place at the center of the action'. For L. Schleiner (1982), the position is even worse than this, since each of the marriages is imposed as a correction to at least one of the partners, rather than as a reward for true lovers. At least one partner – Lucio – is highly reluctant. And so we return once more to Philip Edwards' point that the play's happy ending is 'in spite of the evidence'.

It is certainly worth mentioning the argument of E.A.J. Honigmann's 1981 British Council Lecture, that the virtue of the play lies in the breadth and inclusiveness of its variety: of conflicting feelings, different views of the same person, realistic and folk-tale elements; all of which 'mystifies and keeps changing direction, both at the level of story and of seriousness, insisting on our revising our expectations to the very last'. Jean E. Howard also insists that Shakespeare is intent on a deliberate destabilisation of audience expectations (1983).

Yet, none of this makes for a comfortable play, or for what Northrop Frye claims is the basic celebratory nature of *Measure for Measure*: its capacity, as he argues, to 'contain, instead of merely avoiding, a tragic action'. For Frye, what we see in this play is a 'myth of deliverance, with some resemblances to the myths of deliverance we already know, more particularly the Christian ones'; a resolution achieved by not only annulling or overriding irrational laws or human destructiveness, but 'transcending' them (1983).

It is probably only at the transcendental level that such claims can be made. On any other level, the play remains disturbingly fragmented, populated by characters alien to the spirit of comedy, and pushed into a happy ending against its native grain.

J.A. Bryant voices the only kind of optimism which could be generally accepted of the play, and it is a meagre optimism indeed: 'the comic action does not promise redemption for Vienna, merely survival ... the hope for the community, which is the hope for comedy everywhere, lies in the possibility that a residual charity in some human beings may be appealed to, and that men and women may on occasion give up their charades and accept one another in the kind of love of which the human race at its best is capable' (1986).

II   Text and context: the study of the play's historical environment

In the Joe Papp Central Park production of *Measure for Measure*, the audience roared with laughter when Isabella said the lines, 'Then, Isabel, live chaste, and brother, die:/ "More than our brother is our chastity"'. Evidently, for a 1985 New York audience, the idea of a woman valuing her chastity, particularly with her brother's life at stake, was ludicrous in the extreme.

Actually, modern literary theory teaches that the literary text, far from being sacredly fixed in meaning, is the product of the relationship between itself, its receiver, and various possible contexts. Drama, more than most literary media, is transmitted through multiple agencies and contexts before or even as it reaches its audience: director, set, actor, makeup, fellow audience-member. Far from the Central Park audience response being in any sense impermissible, it modestly illustrates how we each 'de-construct' a text. It also proves how perishable each act of deconstruction is. The idea of chastity in an AIDS-threatened world is no longer such a joke.

However, the humble student of the play, unaware that he or she is a deconstructionist, is likely to want guidance: some simple clue for instance as to the 'right' response to chastity in this play. Here, his or her concerns have some common ground with the 'New Historicist' criticism, which studies any literary text as an intrinsic part of a historical context: not simply as an illustration of what a given historical period thought of a given issue, but as a contribution to its own culture's attitudes. The information from such historical research equips us as audiences with at least one area of certainty if what we seek is stable bearings on the shifting and elusive text. Some of these avenues will be entirely new. For instance, few modern readers or playgoers would normally give much thought to the rights of a monarch: yet, previous times were much excited by the topic, and historical reconstruction can enable us to see a literary text as enacting that interest. In other matters, historical criticism may yield a different angle on a modern concern.

The following section of this book will seek to extend our possible responses to the action of *Measure for Measure*, by summarising what research has uncovered concerning three areas of late-sixteenth/early-seventeenth-century thought: chastity, the laws of matrimony, and the rights and fit government of rulers.

Chastity

We might suspect that the Elizabethan age – the age of the Virgin Queen – treated chastity not as a joke or a protection against disease but as an ideal. George Geckle confirms the suspicion (1971), listing Elizabethan eulogies of chastity by the score.

It would be easy therefore to assume that Shakespeare's Isabella would have been as resoundingly praised in his own time as she was by the Victorians, who, like Dowden, tended to think of her as 'the embodiment of conscience', remarkable for her 'virginal strength and severity and beauty'. Yet, historical criticism has proved that chastity was not an absolute virtue for the Elizabethans and Jacobeans; and even that, to them, Isabella may have been lacking as a heroine.

The first issue here is anti-monasticism. By Shakespeare's post-Reformation day, of course, there were no nunneries and monasteries in England. Shakespeare would never have seen a monk or a nun. Absence, however, did not make the heart grow fonder, or stem the patriotic tide of anti-Catholic prejudice. Darryl J. Gless, researching the religious contexts of *Measure for Measure* (1979), proves that anti-monasticism was part of the air of ideas that Shakespeare breathed.

Gless quotes authorities ranging from Luther and Erasmus to Elizabethan zealots like Thomas Becon, to whom monastic houses seemed 'prisons of antichrist'. Particularly repugnant to them was the 'legalism' of monastic life, the inward-turning recoil from their fellow men, and their claim to dispense salvation. Luther saw monks and nuns as claiming, 'I am Christ', by their pretensions to unusual purity, their presumption that they could dispense forgiveness of sins, and their insistence that salvation could be purchased through rules, gifts, and penances.

Against such a background of hostility, it is by no means clear that, in choosing to make his heroine not merely a sister, but a Sister, Shakespeare chose an admirable stereotype. Chastity might indeed be valued by Shakespeare's times, but apparently professional virgins were not. Nor does Isabella's behaviour temper the usual response. Gless is one of many who call attention to the crucial line where Isabella asks her future Mother Superior, 'And have you nuns no further privileges?' As she hastens to explain, she speaks 'not as desiring more,/ But rather wishing a more strict restraint/ Upon the sisterhood, the votaries of St Clare' [I.iv.1–5]. These lines, to Gless, illustrate her uncharitable flight from the world, and her belief in salvation through her own severity, rather than God's grace.

Incidentally, we ought to be aware that this is an accusation risked not only by Isabella but by Angelo. He, too, sets great store by his chastity. In his case, it is non-monastic, but even more clearly arrogant. In scarcely 'confessing/ That his blood flows; or that his appetite/ Is more to bread than stone' [I.iii.51–3], Angelo, as Gless instructs us, indicates his belief that he is equal with Christ in the wilderness, refusing the temptation to turn stones into bread.

Accordingly, for Gless, Angelo and Isabella do little more than fulfil a quite satisfying pattern of pride brought low: Angelo falling to sexual temptation through Isabella; and Isabella failing her own spiritual test by her insistence on her own chastity above her brother's life. In her tongue-lashing fury at his terrified wish to live, in particular, she demonstrates a vengefulness which is the antithesis to the essential Christian virtue of charity.

Source studies supply valuable reinforcement to this theme. Anne Barton, for instance, points out (1974) that Whetstone's 'Cassandra', the immediate source-figure for Isabella, like all the other source-figures before her, but unlike Isabella, agrees to sacrifice herself for her brother and is praised as a 'chaste lady' and 'virtuous'. The word 'chaste' in connection with sexual violation is somewhat puzzling, until we remember (see J. Rosenheim (1984)) St Augustine's doctrine that a chaste mind can remain intact, even when the body is violated. R.G. Hunter adds the more recent theories of Montaigne – a French writer familiar to English readers – that there could be circumstances in which female submission to violation would be the highest virtue.

Recent feminist criticism, notably the brilliant work of Lisa Jardine (1983), has thrown new light on submission as an Elizabethan/Jacobean ideal. Jardine argues that the familiar male ambivalence about women's attractiveness, and in particular the 'guilt imputed to the female sex for the lust they passively arouse', was particularly strongly marked in this period. Richard Wheeler (1981) adds that the literature of the period is full of instances of the 'imaginary spectral woman, outside the masculine idea of law, who seduces, betrays, castrates'. Correspondingly, the stereotypes of female virtue, the legendary heroines which that age could admire, are all, as Lisa Jardine says, patterns principally of suffering; of 'nobility in adversity'. These figures were found in compilations like *The Golden Legend*, or the recent popular volumes for the edification of women like Painter's *Palace of Pleasure*, 'in which women are the main protagonists, rewarded for their virtues, chastened for their misdemeanours, and acquiescing with gratifying resignation to their (deserved) punishments'.

One of these paragons was the figure of Lucrece. A woman whose entire emotional life depended on her husband, her distress at his absence inflamed the lust of the Roman king Tarquin, who raped her. She made her husband and father vow vengeance, and then stabbed herself to death. As Jardine remarks, it is possible to interpret her suicide as more than a preference of death to dishonour. Rather, it involves an act of self-punishment, for having provoked the tyrant's lust: 'The most powerful stereotypes of female heroism for the Renaissance all involve sexuality chastened in one form or another.'

However, the Lucrece figure first inspires and surrenders to lust before killing herself. Alan Corre (1981), who has discovered somewhat similar stories to *Measure for Measure* but of Judaic origin, notes that in the Judaic versions, it is essential that the woman does not submit to any proposition: here, the woman 'displays Jewish virtue. She is chaste at all costs.' Corre contrasts this with the situation in Cinthio or its ultimate ancestor in St Augustine's *Homily on the Lord's Sermon on the Mount*, in which the virtuous woman displays Christian virtue. She is obedient to her husband's or brother's desires, and, 'in accordance with Pauline doctrines, does not exercise power over her own body but meekly delivers it, as appropriate'. Christopher Palmer's well-meaning indignation (1978) about the selfishness of Claudio, who, like so many other men, 'in the last analysis have one expectation of women: that they submit', is therefore misplaced. Claudio's attitude is the attitude of an entire age, whose standards Isabella fails to measure up to. By those standards, it is she, not Claudio, who would be convicted of selfishness. She is prepared to die, but the age expected its heroines also to surrender their bodies.

This is precisely the step that Isabella refuses to take. She comes close to the stereotype of the virtuous female inspiring lust, but flatly refuses the stereotype of silent suffering. Firstly, Isabella is far from silent. Rosalind Miles (1976) says that Isabella is untypically strident for a heroine of this period, inviting comparison with the various immoral or corrupt scolds of contemporary literature. Secondly, 'were Isabella a Lucretia', says Lisa Jardine (1983) (and the similarities are extremely close in the two stories), she would submit to enforced sex, tell all afterwards, and kill herself'. Jardine concludes, that Isabella is 'belittled by the stereotypes she so flagrantly refuses to match up to'. Her vocation as nun ideally equips her for martyrdom, but she declines the role.

However, Rosalind Miles, criticising Isabella for the 'note of self-congratulation' in her ultimate admission that Angelo was possibly a sincerely chaste man ' 'til he did look on me' [V.i.444], is probably too harsh. Actually, Isabella's admission that she – however unwittingly – in some sense 'created' Angelo's lust is in keeping with what Lisa Jardine writes about the stereotype heroine's willingness to accept blame for the sexuality she inspires. At the end of the play, Isabella may have been chastened into something closer to the ideal.

Elizabethan law on betrothal and marriage

Elizabethan marriage law is not only startling in itself, but of considerable importance to an understanding of some aspects of *Measure for Measure*. A clearer understanding of how the Elizabethans regarded a 'betrothal' (in modern terms, an 'engagement'), or what they thought constituted a 'marriage', will help us to understand what they might have thought about the fantasy-law in the play which sentences Claudio to death; and what they might have thought of the 'bed-trick' which cleverly reunites Mariana with the fiancé who had rejected her. If we can arrive at the conclusion that, for the Elizabethans, Claudio's very willing act with Juliet and Angelo's unknowing act with Mariana (Angelo thinks the act is with Isabella) are in any way equivalent in law, then this has considerable bearing on our response to the comic pattern at large, and the character and the contrivances of the Duke in particular.

The first startling fact of Elizabethan marriage law is how almost ridiculously, appallingly, easy it was to become married.

Where a modern society demands the full involvement of the state and often also wishes the participation of the church before a couple can be recognised as married, for two Elizabethan lovers, all it took was that they made a promise of marriage and then made love. They were then legally married, and could not be unmarried, since divorce was an extraordinary rarity, needing remarkable measures such as an Act of Parliament.

The most thorough work in this area, improving on earlier studies by Harding and Nagarajan, is that of Karl P. Wentersdorf (1979). He points out of course that the 'promise-plus-sex' law was by no means accepted as the ideal mode of marriage. Lawyers were much perplexed by various problems of legitimacy, inheritance and dowries arising out of irregular marriages. The church did much preaching against them. The 'guilty' couple's marriage would be pronounced 'illicit' and their union sinful. They might even undergo punishments under canon law. Yet their marriage would nevertheless still be considered valid.

This was because, traditionally, the essence of a marriage lay not in its sacerdotal recognition in the house of God, but in the union of love in the couple themselves. This was still the opinion of English authorities at the time of *Measure for Measure*. Darryl Gless (1979) quotes from Henry Swinburne's *Treatise of Spousals* (published 1686, but written in 1600): 'it is the consent alone of the parties whereby this knot is tied ... being the very substance (and as it were the life and soul) of this contract'. This clearly validates even an irregular marriage, and Wentersdorf lists cases to support this.

In scholarship in this area over the last forty years there has been much preoccupation with the two basic variants of an irregular marriage: the contract *per verba de praesenti*, and the contract *per verba de futuro*. The distinction was a real one in canon law. It refers to the difference between a betrothal in which the couple promise to marry in the future, and a betrothal in which the couple at that very moment take each other as man and wife. The earlier work of Nagarajan, Schanzer, and Harding often pivots on this nice legal distinction.

However, A.D. Nuttall (1975), again quoting Swinburne's *Treatise*, reminds us that the distinction was in practice often meaningless since, 'to the vulgar sort, "I will take thee" can mean either future or present'. The distinction is anyway annihilated by intercourse, which immediately converts a *de futuro* contract into a *de praesenti* one. Nor were any form of witnesses needed for the marriage to be valid, as Gless, once more quoting Swinburne, establishes.

As a result of this highly permissive law, Nuttall remarks, there was a huge 'disparity between the absolute and indissoluble character of the bond, and the casualness with which it could be formed'. As Biondello in Shakespeare's *The Taming of the Shrew* tells us, 'I knew a wench married in an afternoon as she went to the garden for parsley to stuff a rabbit'. Shakespeare had close acquaintance with the quirks of English marriage law. As Wentersdorf has discovered, he had a good friend who married a widow clandestinely so that she could keep property which would otherwise revert to her family.

Clearly, then, when Claudio tells Lucio, 'upon a true contract/

I got possession of Julietta's bed./ You know the lady, she is fast my wife' [I.ii.144–6], he is merely stating the legality of his marriage under current English law. Promise and act made them man and wife.

Yet, the setting of Shakespeare's play is not England but Vienna, and Vienna is represented as a Catholic state, prepared to enact savage laws against copulation. There is nothing in the play to suggest that Claudio's marriage is illegal even by Viennese standards, but the authorities regard it as sinful and deserving of punishment.

Margaret Scott (1982) argues that this reflects the literal position of Catholic countries in Shakespeare's time. The Tridentine Decree of the Council of Trent, 1563, ruled that irregular marriages had to be subsequently ratified by the church, or were fornicatory.

This was not the case in England, yet there were puritanical reformers who would undoubtedly have acted with the utmost severity against fornicators, including 'married' fornicators, had the law permitted them to do so. R.G. Hunter (1965) and Ronald B. Bond (1985) both quote the sixteenth- and seventeenth-century zealots, Becon, Stubbes, and others, on how lightly 'whoredom' was currently treated ('two or three days in a white sheet before the congregation, and that sometimes not past an howre or two in a day'); and how severely they would like to treat it (to 'tast of present death as God's word doth commaunde'). Bond points out that, when the Puritans came to power after the Civil War, they did indeed enact a law making adultery a capital offence. Hunter and Bond both interestingly speculate that part of Shakespeare's purpose was to depict in Vienna the kind of chaotic situation which men and women would have to live under, if the Puritans were given their way: situations in which basically good people would be put to death, while pimps got off free (see also Foakes (1971)); and in which the law's enforcers were more than likely to break the law themselves.

Claudio and Juliet, therefore, who would be regarded as duly wed if not quite respectably so under English law, are, it seems, threatened with the ludicrous penalties that the Puritans demanded, under the make-believe Draconian law of Vienna; and Shakespeare's purpose is partly an attack on the inhumanity and absurdity of the Puritans' case.

All this has interesting repercussions on the situation of

Angelo and Mariana. They too had vowed to marry, this time in a *de futuro* contract: Angelo was 'affianced to her by oath, and the nuptial appointed' [III.i.215–16]. In the meantime her dowry was lost, and he repudiated her. Yet, when the Duke arranges that Mariana should substitute for Isabella in the 'bed-trick', he is therefore arranging for two people who were betrothed to now sleep together. Under current English law, therefore, since both promise and act were present, the Duke's ploy made Angelo and Mariana man and wife. As Margaret Scott points out, the situations of Claudio-and-Juliet and Angelo-and-Mariana then become legally identical. Both are married, irregularly.

It is therefore a situation rich in irony. The rigorous judge who sentenced Claudio to death, not only turns out to feel the same appetites, but himself commits exactly the same offence. And the Duke who appoints Angelo to enforce the severe laws which he himself let slip now contrives that his strict judge should break the same laws.

James I and ideal kingship

The new king, James I, came down from Scotland to an eager reception. It was partly created by his own little book, *Basilikon Doron*, popularly known as the 'king's book', published in Edinburgh in 1599, but revised, immediately on Queen Elizabeth's death, and sold in such huge numbers that the presses could not keep up with demand. Josephine Waters Bennett (1966) points out that one pirated edition sold three thousand copies and that there were 'several unrecorded editions by other printers'.

The book set out, in the form of James's advice to his heir, the qualities of the ideal ruler: kingship is founded both on the king's authority as God's deputy, but also on the king's own obedience to God's laws. The first duty of a king is therefore a virtuous personal life. On this foundation, he must then rule with justice and mercy, protecting godly ways. As R.J. Schoeck (1980) notices, these ideals are close to the traditional notion neatly summarised in the title of E.H. Kantarowitz's book, *The King's Two Bodies*: that the ruler has two identities; one his mortal identity as one more human being, the other his sacred identity as anointed ruler and as God's representative. King James simply stressed that only by achieving perfection in the first could a king such as himself attain virtue in the second. The implied claim that he actually did exemplify the first was not lost on his new subjects, who expected much from him, but who were also being given a valuable cue. Bennett makes the plausible claim that the 'king's book' was intended to provide the raw material, the 'key note, for all compliments intended to flatter King James'. James was in effect telling his own subjects the most pleasing ways to flatter him.

It has long been believed that this is exactly what Shakespeare was setting out to do. David Lloyd Stevenson (1966) puts much stress on the fact that *Measure for Measure* was actually performed at court at Christmas, at the end of the first full year of James's reign. His argument is that James, seeing the play at court, would have recognised the Duke within the play as a flattering portrait of himself. Stevenson efficiently lists the main resemblances, beginning with the Duke's speech, 'He who the sword of heaven will bear', a speech isolated by the very different, stiff, almost prophetic qualities of its verse, and by its special position at the end of Act III. It is a speech which fully reflects James's own exalted sense of the character of a ruler such as himself. The entire plot might be said to enact James's conviction that a good ruler had to be a good man, or could not claim to enforce the laws against others. This is indeed the doctrine that Angelo, the judge, bases his authority on, though later of course he falls by these same standards.

High among the other parallels found by Stevenson is the stress on cunning statecraft. For the Duke, it is a question, from this same speech at the end of Act III onwards, of applying 'craft against vice'. As one historian has said, James's 'favorite sport, next to hunting, was diplomacy'. Elizabeth Pope (1949) points out that James in *Basilikon Doron* urged his son to 'spy carefully upon [his people's] proceedings'. Even the idea of a ruler in disguise has some parallel in James's experience: his grandfather, the Scots king James V, was 'famous for going among his people incognito' (Bennett).

If James liked 'craft', it must surely partly have been because his own temperament was private and scholarly; and indeed, his hatred of crowds rapidly became something of a legend. Bennett quotes contemporary accounts of his coronation ceremony, which apparently he hurried through so fast that 'a great part' of the speeches 'were left unspoken'. This has its obvious parallel in the speech of the Duke in the play's first scene: 'I love the

people,/ But do not like to stage me to their eyes' [I.i.67–8].
Jonathan Goldberg (1983) quotes a passage in the *Basilikon Doron*,
exactly parallel to this, in which James laments that 'a king is one
as set upon a stage'.

J.E. Price finds multiple references in the play to the subject
of slander. He especially notes the Duke's sensitivity to the
slanderous accusations of Lucio (a character not in the sources,
but Shakespeare's own invention) and his harsh handling of Lucio
at the end of the play, and finds that this strongly-marked trait
has its echo in James's own violent dislike of slander against a
monarch, everywhere evident in *Basilikon Doron*.

The Duke's excessive leniency, his confession to Escalus
that he has neglected to enforce laws, and that his generosity
has been abused, seems to be patterned on James's confession
in *Basilikon Doron* that he had intended 'by being gracious at the
beginning', to win men's hearts; but later found 'the disorder of
the countrie, and the loss of my thanks to be all my reward'.

Finally, there is even a parallel to the Duke's manipulation of
the processes of justice in Act V, his pretence to condemn Angelo,
or Escalus, or Lucio, only to reprieve them later. In 1603 Lord
Cobham and others had plotted with Spanish agents to replace
James with his Catholic cousin Arabella. The plot was discovered,
and James signed the conspirators' death-warrants. However, he
also signed reprieves, and gave these to the executioner with the
instruction that they should not be opened until the three men
were on the scaffold, and at the very point of execution. Clearly,
James desired that his clemency in granting life to the three men
should be as theatrically heightened as possible, by making it a
last-minute rescue.

In every item, then, resemblances between the Duke and
James I can be found. The monarch watching the play would
recognise a portrait of himself; and, as Bennett says, he 'must
have been delighted'.

Yet, Terrell L. Tebbetts (1985) argues that the undoubted
parallel was not intended to be flattering. Between the lines,
Tebbetts argues, we can detect a subtle but audacious attack on
the kind of government – especially government by subterfuge
and manipulation – that James stands for. A fuller discussion of
the basis of Tebbetts's arguments, however, must await the more
general discussion of critical responses to Shakespeare's Duke,
in the next section.

III   Theme and character

Equity

The issue of 'equity' has somewhat slipped out of sight in recent criticism on the play. Yet, the middle way which equity represents between harsh and lax law-enforcement, Ernest Schanzer says, was much on the minds of the Jacobeans (1965). He quotes from a specific work, Perkins's *Treatise of Christian Equity and Lenity*, published in the same year as *Measure for Measure*, which directly identifies equity as that middle way. He points out similar passages in James I's own *Basilikon Doron*. Clearly, too, *Measure for Measure* focuses on a middle way between the over-generous laxity of the Duke's former regime, and the over-harsh severity of Angelo's new one. A small group of scholars have therefore claimed that the play's main theme is a plea in favour of equity.

Schanzer points out a passage in Aristotle's *Nichomachean Ethics*, which formed the basis of all Elizabethan thinking on the issue. Aristotle defined equity as 'a rectification of legal justice'; in other words, equity tempers and softens the strict letter of the law. Wilbur Dunkel and John W. Dickson [both 1962] both remind us that there were specific legal provisions in the Elizabethan judicial system for the principle of equity: the Court of Chancery, administered by the Lord Chancellor. It operated as the merciful voice of the king, and functioned as a court of appeal, or as a means of active intervention by the crown. These interventions were often unpopular with lawyers since they impinged on the supremacy of the common law, and especially since the Court of Chancery operated without a jury system. Yet, Chancery offered a genuine second chance to correct injustices, and Dickson points out that Shakespeare's own father had brought a suit to Chancery.

According to Dickson, the mild judge Escalus, who enforces the law against the multiple offender Mistress Overdone [III.ii.184–6], but merely warns off Pompey (who has never before appeared before Escalus and against whom there is no proper case), is the perfect example of equity in action. Dunkel praises Escalus, yet goes on to claim that the best representative of equity in the play is the Duke himself, as he finally tempers the rigours of the laws he enforces.

More broadly, Schanzer agrees with older critics who feel that what finally emerges out of the bad phases of excessive leniency and harshness is 'a finer justice, based on . . . the true condition of men and things', which the principle of equity represents. This for him, is one of the two major themes in the play.

Mercy

'Mercy' is far broader than equity. Mercy is not an adjustment to the law. It is a higher thing than the law. Intimately tied in with the central doctrines of Christianity, it echoes the divine promise of forgiveness. It gives the offender *better* than he deserves.

As G. Wilson Knight notes (1930), the very title of Shakespeare's play is taken from a central Christian text, the Sermon on the Mount (Matthew 7:1–2): 'judge not, that ye be not judged. For with what measure ye mete it shall be measured to you again'. Ever since Wilson Knight's influential essay, the play has drawn Christian interpretations. Knight himself finds 'an atmosphere of Christianity' and sees the Duke as both 'mystical', 'correspondent with Jesus', and as the equivalent to the figure of the Father of the Prodigal Son, or the Lord of the Unmerciful Servant. Angelo corresponds with the pride of the Pharisees. Isabella, urging Angelo to 'Go to [his] bosom', and confess a 'natural guiltiness' like Claudio's [II.ii.136–9], is echoing Jesus telling the Pharisees to throw the first stone only if they are without guilt themselves. In its final forgiveness, the play parallels the Parable of the Two Debtors.

Nevill Coghill (1955) agrees that the play has something of the air of the morality play, or better still a parable. More recently, J.D. Cox (1983) has spelled out numerous morality plays with similar themes of Christ's New Law of Mercy superseding the Old Judaic law of strict Justice, the theme *par excellence* as he sees it of *Measure for Measure*; and L. Schleiner (1982) greatly extends Knight's list of parables which he feels the play echoes.

Other writers however, have claimed more precise affinities with Christian doctrine than this, feeling the play to be an actual allegory of specific Christian teachings. The classic exposition of this viewpoint is found in Roy Battenhouse's essay (1946) on '*Measure for Measure* and the Christian Doctrine of the Atonement'. In it, he claims that the Duke specifically stands for God, and Isabella for Christ. God's plan is to devise a perfect and symmetrical scheme of justice, so that 'like doth quit like' and measure seems to fit measure. Angelo commits the same crime as Claudio, and seems about to die for the offence. But then, Isabella makes mercy supersede mere justice by her unvengeful and sacrificial pardon of him. She also by marrying the Duke seems to represent the Church marrying God. Angelo of course represents the Devil tempting Christ, in his temptation of Isabella; but also represents fallen mankind saved by Christ.

Darryl Gless, less guilty of schematising than the allegorisers, and perhaps mindful of Mary Lascelles's sensible reminder (1953) that, when the Duke is said to be '*like* power divine' [V.i.366], this does not actually mean that he *is* one, more modestly claims (1979) that the Duke merely 'acts in a way analogous to God'. Elsewhere, he defines the similarity: both are 'powerful, beneficent and ubiquitous'; and though of course the Duke is also a simple fallible human being, he is the dramatic equivalent of a benign providence, and his sweeping gestures of forgiveness are the equivalent of the 'divine extravagance'.

All these interpretations serve the valuable function of reminding us that there is an exceptionally dense grouping in this play of religious reference; that its very title and the undoubted presence of questions about justice and mercy remind us of the most central of Christian doctrines; and that therefore the normal processes of comic salvation here take on a distinctively doctrinal aspect. The only problem is whether the doctrines are ably upheld by the characters they are entrusted to.

Angelo

Angelo at least fits well into an allegorical scheme. His very name suggests 'angel', even though this angel falls. Actually, even his initial purity is of a specific and suspect kind. Ernest Schanzer (1965) points out that when Angelo is referred to as 'precise' [I.iii.50], or when he sees himself as a tempted 'saint' [II.ii.180], both words carry an unmistakable association with Puritanism. My own earlier section, 'Elizabethan law on betrothal and marriage', establishes how strongly Puritans detested extra-marital sex, and this too is an identifying feature of

Angelo, who does not recognise sexual desire in himself – 'scarce confesses that his blood flows'; and who, in his second interview with Isabella equates sex – 'coin[ing] heaven's image' – with murder – stealing 'a man already made'. The arrogance of his assumptions here has already been pointed out. J.W. Lever adds that, in seeing his own susceptibility to Isabella in terms of 'saint' tempted by a 'saint', he is putting himself in the same category as St Jerome who was tempted by the devil in the likeness of a virtuous woman.

'Saint' Angelo, however, has already shown a loathsome cruelty to his fiancée Mariana. The Duke tells Isabella the whole distressing story of how, when Mariana's brother was lost at sea, and, with him, Isabella's dowry, Angelo disowned her; the worst part of the story being that, in order to get rid of her, Angelo pretended to have heard about some 'discoveries of dishonour' [III.i.229]; a 'vicious slander', as Donald Gless calls it, which leaves Mariana not only deserted but also unmarriageable.

Partly, then, the whole of the rest of the play might be said to enact Angelo's punishment for his past sins – his pharisaical pride as a Puritan who sets himself up as a saint, or as the equal of Christ in the Wilderness; and of course also to punish his further sins as virgin-violator, once he is aroused by Isabella.

Actually, many commentators have pointed out that his 'fall' is part of his punishment: the man who had despised lust above all things now finds himself lust's victim. Rosalind Miles (1976) describes the sheer surprise of the discovery for him; and on the 'amazement, disgust and grief' expressed in the soliloquies of II.ii and II.iv, his 'babble of terrified questions, the broken rhythms of these speeches'. In effect, it is his entire self-image which here collapses.

Nevertheless, one of the sufferers is still Isabella. Here, Angelo at first approaches carefully. He sets rhetorical traps, and hypothetical questions. He gets her to concede that some sins are worse than others. Supposing there were a way – say, by 'yielding up [her] body to . . . sweet uncleanness' – to 'redeem' her brother's life? (The word 'redeem', Donald Gless argues, seems especially to invite her to equate sexual surrender with Christ's sacrifice for mankind.) Isabella seems not to understand the question. Ernest Schanzer says that Angelo must feel like a chess-player 'who finds his most skilful and calculated moves come to nothing, simply because his opponent fails to understand their purpose and therefore does not reply in the expected manner' (1965). At this point he is compelled to become more crudely obvious in his proposition: and, when she indignantly rejects it, he gives his 'sensual race' its head. She will yield to him, or else Claudio will do more than die: 'but thy unkindness shall his death draw out/ To ling'ring sufferance'. Gless remarks that Angelo's ultimatum is almost crueller than a rape. If raped, Isabella would be sinless. Yet, Angelo demands her complicity: something in between consent and compulsion.

The next we hear of Angelo directly is in Act IV. By now, he believes he has slept with Isabella (though actually, he's slept with his own rejected fiancée Mariana); and yet, in IV.ii.118, he reneges on his side of the bargain, and orders Claudio's immediate execution. The motive he gives, in IV.iv.28, when we next see him, is pure self-protection, in case Claudio later might have 'ta'en revenge'. This is the nadir of Angelo's character in the play, but as Rosalind Miles reminds us, there is still the calculated cynicism of his handling of the accusations of Mariana and Isabella in Act V, and the sinister ring of 'I did but smile till now' [V.i.231]. Only in begging for death, when finally exposed, does he move anything but distaste; but, even here, Northrop Frye (1983) describes him as 'the most contemptible kind of hypocrite, the kind who tries to make himself feel better by despising himself'. Ernest Schanzer cites six separate references calling Angelo either a counterfeit coin (an 'angel' was worth ten shillings) or a devil.

In more modern terms, David Holbrook condemns Angelo as a sex-maniac (1986), and Hans Sachs, in a long psychoanalytical article (1970) gives clinical precision to Holbrook's charge. For Sachs, 'the outstanding trait of his character is cruelty. . . . The normal forms of sexuality are repulsive to him. This [is] why he pursues them with such cold hate. [Instead, he] shows what psycho-analysis calls a sublimation, an outlet for his dark desires. [Even when] his cruelty falls back regressively to its original source, revealing its primary sensual form, the new temptation is still . . . that of sadism.'

Angelo's flaws are indeed so manifest that Dr Johnson disapproved of his final acquittal: 'I believe every reader feels some indignation when [Angelo] is spared.' Certainly, as J.W. Lever (1965) remarks, Angelo's recognition that death is his just desert 'removes the irony of his declaration to Escalus:

When I that censure him do so offend,
Let mine own judgement pattern out my death,
And nothing come in partial.   [II.i.29–31]

The sense of a pattern of just desert is very symmetrical in this respect. Yet, F.R. Leavis (1952) urges us to 'see ourselves in Angelo', and reminds us that Isabella's words, 'Go to your bosom,/ Knock you there [and] confess/ A natural guiltiness such as his' [II.ii.136–9] apply not only to Angelo recognising guilt like Claudio's but to our need to recognise the faults of Angelo in us. If this is so, there is no actual obstruction in Angelo's own character against fitting him into an allegorical scheme such as Roy Battenhouse's. He can indeed be read as an 'angel' that falls and becomes a devilish tempter. He can also be read as a fallen human being like us all, deserving of punishment under the strict rule of law, yet redeemed finally by a higher grace.

Isabella

Stage interpretations of Angelo do not widely differ from each other. The basic type – severe, repressive – admits of few variations. Isabella is another matter. In the Bogdanov production in Canada (1985), she was costumed as a frump, in dowdy skirt and shapeless cardigan. Four years earlier, Brenda Curtis had played her as very cool and refined, still as a marble statue under Angelo's assault. The same year, in Manchester, she emerged as a militant, her costume suggesting a captain in the Salvation Army. In the RSC production in 1983, she was a blend of timidity and impulse, including her final leap to the Duke after his proposal of marriage.

All these characteristics can be found in Isabella. She provides any hostile critic, particularly, with a wealth of ammunition; and there has been no shortage of hostility towards her. Darryl Gless's attack on the spiritual arrogance of her chastity has already been mentioned. J.W. Lever (1965) suggests that, though she pleads for mercy, it is against her true convictions. David Lloyd Stevenson (1966) more bluntly says that 'she is the living antidote to all human charity'. He quotes the comment of an older critic, Arthur Quiller-Couch, that there is something 'rancid' about Isabella's chastity: and Quiller-Couch's allegation that in encouraging Mariana to sleep with Angelo – having indignantly rejected the idea herself – she becomes a 'procuress'. Rosalind Miles describes this same turnaround as 'an unscrupulous readiness to place another head on the block intended for herself', and comments on the bossiness with which she instructs Mariana what to do (1976).

Her lack of ladylike meekness has often been commented on, and Mary Lascelles contrasts her here with the 'sweet compliance' with which Whetstone's heroine accepted her fate in the source-play. In particular, her ferocity against her brother's wish to live – 'O you beast!/ O faithless coward! O dishonest wretch . . . Die, perish . . . I'll pray a thousand prayers for thy death,/ No word to save thee' [III.i.139–50] – has drawn criticisms too numerous to list. Nor has even her earlier skill in arguing for her brother's life escaped condemnation. Bernice Kliman (1982) describes her as 'inept'. Certainly, as Rosalind Miles points out, she makes an extremely nervous and reluctant start, and J.W. Lever remarks on the extremely unusual form that her plea takes. Rather than addressing the mitigating circumstances of Claudio's case – he was, after all, engaged to Juliet, and the act actually made her his wife – she chooses to plead the principle of mercy: that we should 'judge not'. Lever and later Terry Eagleton (1986) in their various ways point out how such a plea 'struck at the very bases of order on which human society rested'; how it was a 'gratuitous rupture of the circuit'.

However, the attack on Isabella's debating skills has recently focused less on the arguments she uses than the way in which she uses them. F.R. Leavis (1952) commented on the 'sensuality of martyrdom' Isabella displays in her chastity. Since 1978, many have taken up the cry. Harriet Hawkins (1978) implies that 'sexuality' might be substituted for Leavis's 'sensuality', and sees Isabella as 'the feminine counterpart of Angelo', not merely in her professed hatred of sex, but in her underlying 'keen appetite'. S. Moore (1982) remarks that Isabella's persuasions to Angelo have a strong unconscious sexual suggestiveness. R.A. Levin (1982) and Ronald Huebert (1983), agreeing, specifically mention her use of the words 'your potency' [II.ii.67], and 'your pleasure' [II.iv.31], in addressing Angelo. However, the most sustained work in this area is by Carolyn E. Brown (1986b), whose whole interpretation of Isabella is as a sexual masochist offering herself in fantasy if not in fact to a sadistic Angelo.

Brown here stresses how Isabella repeatedly puts herself in the posture of helplessness, while flattering Angelo's sense of his own power; how her whole argument for mercy is pitched in terms of the idea that Angelo, too, might find himself capable of sexual desire; and how, altogether, she puts to work skills which her brother describes, more accurately than he knows, as 'a *prone* and speechless dialect/ Such as men move' [I.ii.182–3].

Brown's major concentration, though, is on her response to Angelo's question whether she would lay down her body to save her brother's life:

> . . . were I under the terms of death,
> Th'impression of keen whips I'd wear as rubies,
> And strip myself to death as to a bed
> That long I have been sick for, ere I'd yield
> My body up to shame   [II.iv.100–104]

Brown comments that right up to the 'ere', at the end of the sentence, this reads like an acceptance, not a rejection. Only the last clause reverses the expected drift. She then comments on the language of whips, bed, and sick longings. The descriptive terms clearly convey that, to Isabella, the torture seems desirable: 'the bloody stripes on the skin glow like rare precious gems', and the rape would be merely a 'yield[ing], not a repulsive violation'. Again, the word 'impression' implies softness, and 'keen whips' a sharp penetration. In all, Isabella 'graphically envisions the beating scene'. Richard Levin adds interesting corroboration to this theory, when he notices how her later speech on breaking glass and soft complexions [II.iv.125–30] stresses a female weakness, passively inviting male force.

These interpretations of Isabella have one welcome bonus. They make sense of one of the play's most implausible transitions: Angelo's transformation from Puritan to lecher. If we credit the theories of Angelo's own sexual desire being powerful but repressed, we can also accept that Isabella, in her innocent suggestiveness, her inadvertent invitation for him to violate her, 'acts as a stimulus to Angelo's overwrought imagination' as Rosalind Miles says (1976). In fact, in her combined purity and defenceless sexuality, she is precisely the one type of woman who would arouse Angelo's repressed and sadistic lust.

Naturally, Isabella's defenders tend not to stress this dimension in her. One very persistent defence they offer is that Isabella is in reality neither fanatic nor pervert, but merely a frightened girl. Josephine Waters Bennett describes her (1966) as a 'young girl, inexperienced'. This especially applies to Isabella's famous wish that the nunnery she plans to enter, the order of St Clare (notable, as Bennett reminds us, for the strictness of its rule), had even 'a more strict restraint' [I.iv.4]. Bennett describes her here as no more than 'a romantic schoolgirl'. Rosalind Miles agrees: it is 'the manifestation not of a natural coldness and repressiveness, but of self-ignorance and inexperience'. Ralph Berry (1981) concludes that the inverted commas in her famously frigid lines at the end of Act II, 'Then, Isabel, live chaste, and, brother, die./ "More than our brother is our chastity" ', denote a 'falling back upon a moral maxim . . . in great mental distress'. As to her subsequent rage at her brother's reluctance to die, J.W. Lever points out that this is 'her second male solicitation in a short space of time' from sources she had trusted; first Angelo, now Claudio. As Lever points out, she had above all relied on her brother to rescue her from the dilemma Angelo had placed her in; and she was willing to modify her previous horror of his 'vice' [II.ii.29] to a toleration of his mere 'prompture of the blood' [II.iv.178], if only he would save her chastity. As Mary Lascelles comments, Isabella's state of mind in her dilemma is one of pure 'terror'. When Claudio too betrays her, Northrop Frye remarks (1983), she is 'totally demoralised'. It is small wonder that she accepts any way out, including the one offered by the Duke to substitute Isabella. She is, of course, as Josephine Bennett points out, a novice nun, eager to accept the authority of a Friar.

Much finally depends on our attitude to Isabella's last phase, where she accuses Angelo in public, yet finally kneels, at Mariana's request, to beg mercy for him. This is one of the play's essential moments, and her gesture carries the play's full theme of mercy superseding justice. Her behaviour here has not entirely escaped criticism. It was Dr Johnson who first accused her of vanity, in her speech, 'I partly think/ A due sincerity governed his deeds/ Till he did look on me': 'I am afraid our Varlet Poet intended to inculcate, that women think ill of nothing that raises the credit of their beauty, and are ready, however virtuous, to pardon any act which they think incited by their charms'. Rosalind Miles (1976) echoes the charge two centuries later with her reference to Isabella's 'inadvertent note of self-congratulation'. Anne Barton comments on the illogicality of her plea that Angelo's 'act did not o'ertake his bad intent'. True, Angelo had not slept with Isabella, but he had slept with Mariana, an act equivalent to the one for which he executed Claudio – or thought he had.

Yet, Josephine Bennett describes this same speech as a 'wonderful speech, wrung from her in grief and understanding. The broken lines and simple, abrupt phrasing suggest how hard they are to say' (1966). The act of pleading on her knees for her enemy certainly crowns the theme of mercy in the play.

Her reward may be the offer of marriage that the Duke makes to her at the end of the play. Yet, our rejoicing at that reward is surely conditional on whether we believe him to be a husband worth having, and this may in turn await the discussion of the Duke in the next section.

Duke Vincentio

Northrop Frye points out that the Duke's role is the largest speaking part in any of Shakespeare's comedies, which of course gives the character an exceptionally strong influence over the play. Michael Scott argues, on the basis of many recent productions, that, to give the play an overall unity, an emphatic interpretation of him – as weakling, divine power, manipulator, or whatever – is an essential. Certainly, criticism has given play directors a whole variety of emphatic interpretations to choose from.

It seems only fair to give the first say to favourable interpretations. His apologists give full value to his functions as caring monarch, or as chief engineer of the ideal of mercy in the play, as other sections of this study emphasise (see 'Text and Context: James I and Ideal Kingship'; and 'Theme and Character: Mercy'). This would make him into an 'ultimately benevolent authority', a 'kindly father', as Rosalind Miles describes him (1976). She stresses the 'deep moral seriousness' of his role, and his place especially in the last phase of the play as the Shakespearean 'battering-ram' against the cruel and limited concept of 'measure for measure'. She rightly points out that he has difficult tasks to perform: 'to make Angelo transcend his genuine and strong

death-wish; . . . to teach Isabella to forgive'. This is of course
the ultimate defence of the Duke's contrivances: he needs them,
if he is to fulfil these lofty and necessary purposes. He must, for
instance, insist that Angelo will die, exactly as Claudio has died,
just so that Isabella's plea for his life will be genuine. He must
thoroughly pretend to be merciless, so as to evoke mercy in others.
S. Moore describes this technique as 'virtuous machiavellianism'
(1982), based on the Duke's 'unshakeable faith in man's ability to
learn before it is too late'. Under the same argument of necessity,
Darryl Gless defends (1979) the Duke's harsh sermon to Claudio,
'be absolute for death' [III.i.5–41]. Admittedly, it contains no iota
of the Christian doctrine of salvation, which is odd for even a
make-believe Friar. Yet, Claudio was suffering, Gless points out,
from the sin of 'excessive attachment to life'. In accordance with
the discipline of the 'art of dying', the Duke merely corrects
Claudio, to the point where, because 'he no longer loves it,
Claudio is prepared for life in this world'.

Yet, even Vincentio's defenders seem often to remain dissatis-
fied with him. There is a frequent strain of complaint about his
apparent cold remoteness. Rosalind Miles (1976) remarks on the
lack of any 'emotional interaction' with those he saves. Richard
Wheeler (1981) describes Vincentio as 'aloof . . . bereft of inner
life . . . a void at the heart of the play'. He astutely remarks
on the danger of such a distanced figure, apparently without
any human ties, in a play whose major theme – 'judge not' –
stresses the 'shared core of human experience'. Translated into
the theatre, for instance in Peter Brook's 1979 Paris production,
the Duke becomes distinguished primarily, as Wolfgang Sohlich
argues (1984), by an 'esthetic disposition; a polite ruler but
essentially remote from those he rules'. These more recent critics
echo the comments of Mary Lascelles (1953) or W.W. Lawrence
(1931) on the 'failure of engagement' in Vincentio, or his status
as an 'artificial figure'. Cynthia Lewis (1983) expresses a very rare
view in finding him 'progressively engaged' during the course of
the action.

So pronounced is this characteristic that David Lloyd Stevenson
(1966) expresses some relief at the Duke's failings, since these at
least humanise him. Of these failings, the very least accusation
is P.S. Spinrad's (1984), that he is a typical official, wanting
to be loved in office: hence his delegation of an unpleasant
and unpopular job to Angelo. Again, this touch of vanity is

echoed in modern productions: for instance in the 1983 Royal Shakespeare Company version, which gave the Duke a gigantic mirror to pose in.

More damaging is the accusation that Angelo's remoteness is less royal than prudish. What is so harmful about this charge is its implication that this Duke, whose eventual function in the play is to soften and to humanise, is at heart guilty of exactly the same sins he corrects; to be precise, the sins of priggish superiority to the failings of others.

Cynthia Lewis (1983) sees this as an initial trait of the Duke. N.W. Bawcutt (1984) sees it as pervasive. Bawcutt takes as his cue the Duke's confession that he wishes he had punished more harshly in the past [I.iii.35–9]. He speaks of the 'biting' law (Carolyn Brown (1986a) suspects the Duke's flagellatory obsession here); and, when he does intervene to mitigate it, it is only when Angelo's severity is found to be hypocritical. The Duke's speech at the end of Act III is notable for its regret that Angelo was not indeed 'as holy as severe'. The regret is not at the severity, but only at the lack of holiness. This seems to substantiate R.G. Hunter's earlier theory (1965) that, up to this point, the Duke 'had been willing to accept provisionally Angelo's ethic of repression and/or death as a solution'. Richard Wheeler goes further, and argues that the Duke deliberately chose Angelo, so that he could experience the pattern of seething vice and sadistic punishment as a voyeur; the horror being as much desired as abhorred. The Duke's fundamental attitude is therefore not – as is usually supposed – one of opposition to his deputy, but one of identification with him (1981). According to L. Schleiner (1982), he is thoroughly a 'man of tests', resorting to mercy only when the results prove catastrophic.

Thereafter, according to some critics, his motives are less idealistic than cynical. Inga-Stina Ewbank (1984) points out that the Duke's ethic is that the end justifies the means, in his description of the 'bed-trick' to Isabella: 'the doubleness of the benefit defends the deceit from reproof' [III.i.257–8]. Richard Wheeler objects that this device in effect makes him a bawd, just as much as the low-life figure of Pompey, whom the Duke verbally flays in the very next scene ('a bawd, a filthy bawd . . . a filthy vice' [III.ii.17–25]). Ewbank neatly points out that the Duke's 'bed-trick' involves Isabella in lying to Angelo about lying with him. Others, like Rosalind Miles, comment on the 'gratuitous nature of his manoeuvres', when he decides that, 'craft against vice I must apply' at the end of Act III. Even the normally-sympathetic Darryl Gless convicts him of 'sinful mendacities'.

Worse, the mendacities do not even work very effectively, particularly when he begins his manipulations. Things go wrong. As Anne Barton says (1974), he is 'continually surprised by the unpredictability, not to mention rank insubordination, of his elected cast of characters'. Schleiner stresses the unwillingness of the human material to be saved, and sees this as a comic feature of the play. Certainly, as Rosalind Miles says, it is difficult to resist the idea of comedy when the Duke is caught so completely napping by Angelo's decision (though believing he has had Isabella) to execute Claudio anyway; and Miles draws our attention to the crowning comedy of the Duke's plan to use the murderer Barnadine's head as a substitute for Claudio's, on the theory that 'death's a great disguiser' [IV.ii.170]. When Barnadine understandably declines the kind offer, the Duke's impotent fury – 'Unfit to live, or die: O gravel heart' [IV.iii.62] – provides a hilarity matched only by his pious rejoicing – 'O, 'tis an accident that Heaven provides!' [75] – when told that a head is after all available; to whit, the pirate Ragozine's, conveniently dead in the jail from a fever that very morning.

Yet, this is far from the end of the case against Vincentio. There are many who not only convict him of manipulative and ineffectual means in a virtuous cause, but who accuse him even of acting in corrupt causes. Again, to take the least first, there is H.R. Coursen's accusation of 'image-mongering' (1984); of engineering a grand finale to demonstrate how he has rescued the country (from 'problems he himself has promoted'). Again, productions tend to stress this aspect of the play, by using various obvious symbols of power, such as in the Belgian National Theatre production in 1981 with its huge thrones. Terrell Tebbetts (1985) agrees, seeing Vincentio's sudden imposition of the old laws, through Angelo, as an artificial act, designed to promote himself, finally, as a kind of 'saviour of the people from the law'. Leonard Tennenhouse, working on the parallel of King James's own patriarchal tamperings with his state, likewise argues (1982) that all Vincentio's ploys serve only to reaffirm the ruler's power.

For several critics, the Duke here has a very specific political supremacy to prove: his authority over Angelo. R. Hillman (1986) describes Angelo as Vincentio's 'rival for eminence' and Vincentio's schemes as being directly designed, not for his salvation, but for his 'humiliation'. Interestingly, W.W. Lawrence had half-a-century previously noticed how Vincentio seems almost to avoid Angelo between Acts I and V. To R.A. Levin (1982), this is so that he can finally 'prove himself unlike Angelo by stepping in to judge his deputy and right his deputy's wrongs'. Levin and many others stress the blockbuster nature of Act V, the massive and public nature of the final unveilings. Dennis Kay comments on the unusually huge concentration of information in the Duke's own hands, unlike the usual comic convention of an exchange of information. Some writers, like Marcia Riefer (1984), see him here as the writer/producer/director of his own 'carefully devised playlet', revelling in his own virtuosity. Once more, acted versions of the play seem to concur: notable here is the 1981 Wisconsin Shakespeare Festival production which inserted a choreographed masque as prologue to the play, with the Duke as director/spectator of both this and the main action.

Finally, there are those who see the Duke's actions as suspect, even in relation to Isabella. Prominent here is Marcia Riefer's argument that the entire action is designed to promote patriarchal authority at the expense of women.

Riefer argues that, while many male figures temporarily evade the Duke's authority (Angelo, Lucio, Barnadine), neither Mariana nor Isabella is permitted independence. Indeed, the Duke gives Isabella a subservient role, to work Mariana over to the 'bed-trick'. It is a role which involves her also in going back to Angelo, and promising him her body. Angelo had commanded Isabella to 'put on the destin'd livery' of a 'woman' (i.e. of female sexuality [II.iv.138, 135]). Now, symbolically at least, Vincentio makes her do exactly that. Janet Adelman's note to the BBC production of the play points out that this is precisely what Isabella had tried to avoid, by adopting her nun's habit. Vincentio in effect forces her to abandon her retreat from male power, just as Mariana is abruptly compelled to leave the protected limbo of her 'moated grange', and take a husband. Richard Wheeler goes on to argue that Isabella's 'symbolic defilement' is still more pronounced in Act V; when the Duke commands her, against her will ('To speak so indirectly I am loath' [IV.vi.1]), openly to accuse Angelo of having slept with her. The gesture is certainly not necessary, since Mariana almost immediately after it makes her truthful claim that it was her, not Isabella, that Angelo slept with. 'Isabella then undergoes the added indignity of having her claim regarded as criminal madness and conspiracy.' In all, Wheeler believes that Vincentio's handling of Isabella is characterised by 'aggression', by the need to humble and finally possess her: and Richard Levin makes the intriguing point that, by the end of Act V, Isabella is now doing to the Duke what she once did to Angelo; pleading apparently in vain for a man's life.

Levin adds that the plea is made in both cases to a man who wants her for himself. The difference is that the Duke succeeds in taking her. Admittedly, his chosen means are a respectable offer of marriage; but as R. Hillman (1986) sardonically remarks, the Duke still succeeds in 'getting Angelo's girl'.

These theories interestingly parallel the very sophisticated work of Jonathan Goldberg (1983) on King James I's public and private images. Goldberg tells us that 'beneath [James's] assertions of the inscrutability of the royal will are secret desires and delights'. This pollution of the public by the private, to very crudely paraphrase Goldberg's theories, James tried to disguise, by his idea of the monarch (public figure) as the father (private figure) of his people. Goldberg comments on *Measure for Measure*, and describes the Duke's marriage to Isabella in terms of an asserted dominance: 'the Duke appears to be in Angelo's place, offering redemption to Isabella in exchange for sexual favours; . . . even though he offers marriage, it is at least as much an assault upon her integrity as Angelo's proposition'.

In production, the Duke's offer of marriage has often been handled in far from up-beat ways. As Richard Wheeler explains, the cue for this is in the play itself, in 'the curious silence of those who benefit from the Duke's mercy'. This certainly includes Isabella. The Duke first makes his proposal as he restores her living brother to her: 'Give me your hand and say you will be mine' [V.i.489]. In the face of her silence, he subsequently has to repeat the offer: 'What's mine is yours, and what is yours is mine' [534]. Again he receives only silence. The same silence seems to afflict Claudio himself, Angelo, who is likewise spared from death, and Barnadine, who is somewhat improbably made to undergo a course of religious instruction, 'to provide/ For better times to come' [481–2]. It is Wheeler's theory that the releases are too sudden, from deaths that seemed all too imminent, so that there can as yet be no rejoicing. Three 1981 productions illustrate how the theatre has handled this moment. In the San Francisco Shakespeare Company's production, Isabella was given a long, long hesitation before taking the Duke's hand; Brenda Curtis's Isabella, in the same year, gave her hand instead to her brother; and the Hungarian National Theatre production saw the Duke physically arranging a group of silent, despondent people.

Richard Wheeler elsewhere stresses how the Duke-as-Friar encourages Claudio's sense of sexual shame; how he browbeats Juliet into describing her love as 'an evil' [II.iii.35]; how he forces Angelo into a commission which he does not want, which ends with a coition which 'unshapes [him] quite' [IV.iv.18]. In all, the entire cast has undergone a process of shame. If, as Darryl Gless repeatedly argues, these are necessary processes in the cases of Isabella and Angelo, whose stiff-necked pride needs a humanising fall, the incidental benefit for the Duke is his own total supremacy. By the end of the play almost every major or minor character owes life, status or marriage directly to him.

Lucio

Lucio, an apparently minor figure, turns up often enough in the play to accumulate some 12.3 per cent of the play's speeches, and 11 per cent of its words. Clearly, he has a function. Indeed, various critics have detected several different functions.

There have been occasional attempts to cast him as an evil figure (Matthew Winston (1981) compares him with Lucifer), or as the ultimate truth-teller (Maurice Charney (1985)). Most, though, respond more simply and warmly. He makes us laugh, in a play which contains much serious material. Josephine Bennett points out how he initially lightens this serious material, simply by the irony of function: 'Lucio the libertine, the coach of Isabella the virgin, in a plea for mercy for a fornicator, a plea which arouses the Duke's lust' (1966). Or again in the final scenes, where he 'abuses the Friar to the Duke, as he had previously abused the Duke to the Friar'. This latter point is ably developed by Rosalind Miles (1976), who sees the Duke's Act V toying with Lucio as heavily reinforcing his resumption of power.

The pleasure he gives us is mostly the pleasure we get from any gossip, particularly when directed against the high and mighty. Here, Lucio's special target is the Duke, who, as Ronald Huebert says (1983), is otherwise the one untested figure in the play. Lucio becomes, in Inga-Stina Ewbank's words (1984), a 'kind of safety valve for our ambivalent feelings about the Duke'; or a 'lightning rod against taking the Duke at his own valuation' (Northrop Frye (1983)). As such he often speaks with uncanny accuracy. Clifford Leech obviously hits the target when he says that 'when Lucio refers to "the old fantastical Duke of dark corners" [IV.iii.155–6], he gives us a phrase that our memories will not let go' (1950); the Duke consciously endorses 'craft' and 'falsehood' and behaves accordingly. Similarly, Richard Levin believes (1982) that Lucio's frequent slanders about the Duke's own sexuality ('He's not past it yet' [III.ii.171, etc.]) correspond to the urge in Vincentio to let Angelo 'act out his own repressed desires'.

Arthur C. Kirsch insists (1975) that Lucio's slanders are another link to the master-theme of uncharitable judgement. Yet, a further indication of the grain of truth in these slanders is Vincentio's reaction to them. Jean Howard (1983) and Richard Wheeler (1981) both describe his response as excessively and surprisingly indignant; and J.E. Price (1984) points out the major set-speeches [III.ii.175–9, IV.i.59–64] and many smaller ones, in which the Duke vents his indignation at being slandered. Since the slanders contain an element of truth, Richard Levin argues that our responses to Lucio's final punishment – the threat of whipping and death, commuted to forcible marriage to a whore – are very divided.

Certainly, Lucio had fathered the whore's child. This is entirely in keeping with his sexual morals. Yet, once again, Lucio here offers a voice that partly attracts us. Margaret Scott (1982) argues that the play contains violently antithetical views of sex: 'these filthy vices' on the one hand; 'the sport' on the other. In a play which is packed with characters who tend to the first view, it is predominantly Lucio who expresses the second. In Act III, scene ii, he gives us a barrage of comic metaphors for sex: 'the rebellion of a codpiece', 'a ducat in her clack-dish', or 'eating mutton on Fridays'. Nor is he merely a cynic. He proves a true friend to Claudio (Elizabeth Pope calls him 'gallant and agreeable' (1949)); indeed he is Claudio's salvation. I believe it was E.K. Chambers who once remarked that, but for the energetic promptings of this unprincipled rake, the righteous (Angelo and

Isabella) would have killed Claudio between them. Altogether, his healthy dissent relieves the pious coerciveness of the bulk of the play. Here, he resembles the stubborn Barnadine, whose sole function, says J.W. Lever (1965), is to assert 'that no man's life is so worthless as to be sacrificed to another's convenience'.

Part Two: Appraisal

Measure for Measure will undoubtedly continue to perplex new audiences and readers, and in that sense alone is likely to remain for the foreseeable future in the category of 'Problem Play'. The reason is not hard to find. However intelligently the play is read, or however ably it is produced in the theatre, it confuses us. Comic convention seems to collide with serious content; religious allegory is devalued by plot contrivance; we are asked to respond with a fine moral sensibility at one stage, and then to numb the same responses later on.

Yet, if the spontaneous response will be hard to change, we may see at least a theoretical solution to these difficulties: namely, to ignore the long-established insistence on the play as a moral allegory. So long as we insist that *Measure for Measure* is such an allegory, with the Duke as a 'power divine', complaints against his very fallible playing of this role will continue to be voiced. To silence complaint, it is necessary to view the play and the Duke entirely differently: not as having idealistic goals and failing to meet them, but as successfully pursuing far more worldly goals.

This, it seems to me, is the very crux of the debate on the play, and the basis on which we must make our decisions; particularly, on the presence or otherwise of a predominantly spiritual dimension in it.

Undoubtedly, with its extremely high ratio of Biblical reference, even in its very title, *Measure for Measure* compels us to acknowledge religion as a significant component among its themes. Its *dramatis personae* include nuns and friars, and its chief character disguises as a friar. The play's conclusion seems to act out the Christian message of mercy; a new dispensation replacing the pitiless Old Law. Best of all, perhaps, is that we can clearly see, through Isabella's transformation, that message embodied in a major

character, who learns the meaning of humility, who is brought
to acknowledge her fellowship with fallible humanity, and who
therefore learns to forgive even her enemy. It is this ethic of
mercy which has the last word in the play, overcoming in a very
satisfying way Angelo's call that the justice which he had called
down on others should now fall on his own head.

Yet, it is the Duke who almost single-handedly contrives the
victory of this ethic of mercy in the play. A great deal therefore
depends on whether we can seriously believe in his 'divinity' or
even his moral sincerity. It is worth reminding ourselves of Mary
Lascelles's remark that Vincentio, rather than *being* a 'power
divine' (or even an allegory of it) is simply *compared to* divine
authority by subjects accustomed to paying such tributes. Her
recognition frees us not only to question the Duke's divinity,
but to wonder even about his motives: whether, for instance his
exercise in the ethics of justice and mercy might not turn out to
be no more than a useful part of his experiment in power which
is thoroughly human, and not at all 'divine'.

If it seems that, however spiritually exquisite the outcome
of the play, it was a by-product of other concerns, and that
the Duke's own preoccupations were not spiritual at all, then
religion's presence appears in a much more ambiguous light
than the play's more idealistic interpreters would concede.

The theatre has given us a cue here. From the 1973 Jonathan
Miller production which was set in the Vienna not of the
seventeenth century but of Freud, down to Hugh Landwehr's
1979 Baltimore setting of the play in a sterile white laboratory
space, designers and directors have been drawn to the idea of
experiment; implying that curiosity and the urge to tamper are
truly the impulses motivating the Duke.

The view which this 'Appraisal' will accordingly explore
and then modify is that the play depicts a moral experiment, with the Duke as the experimenter. The idea is not
entirely new. Wilson Knight described Vincentio's scheme as 'a
scientific experiment to see if extreme ascetic righteousness can
stand the test of power'. However, Knight also and illogically
continued to insist on the profound divinity of the Duke's role.
Likewise, F.R. Leavis described the play as 'an experimental
demonstration upon Angelo'; but again, he too insisted on the
religious theme – the experiment was to prove the truth of the
Biblical injunction, 'judge not, that ye be not judged'. Only Anne

Barton has previously seen the experimental element in the play in non-moral terms, in her observation that the Duke displays a scientific curiosity as to how people will behave under stress.

In this view, Vincentio emerges as a true Jacobean moral experimenter; governed by curiosity rather than ethics, and characterised by an irresponsibility entirely true to type. On such a view we no longer require his moral consistency, nor his flawless statesmanship. He is still a 'good' Duke, not a villain, and his manipulations do preserve lives. Yet, he saves them from perils of his own making; dangers to which he himself had deliberately exposed them in the first place. Seen this way, he seems a highly spurious saviour. We may suspect that his motives are detached rather than concerned; or, if we find concern at all, it may be for himself, his own status, and his own amusement. Even as he 'saves' his subjects, we may discern his interest above all in probing, measuring, and discovering how they will respond under the extremest moral test-situations.

Moral experiments in Jacobean drama

If *Measure for Measure* can be interpreted in this way, it would be seen not as unique, but as fitting into a distinct pattern, and a very precise time-scale. As I argue elsewhere (1980, 1988), the beginning of James I's reign saw a startling new interest, in the best plays of the ablest playwrights, in the idea of moral subversion. Earlier plays had of course shown evil men. The difference is that these new plays devise 'heroes' who not only commit evil acts, but who do so from a motive primarily of curiosity. They may also be interested in power or money or revenge, but enquiry is foremeost. They wish to discover how far they can go, morally. They seek to find out if innocence is a reality or a fraud; and so, in actual moral experiments, they devise ways to test their own innocence and that of others. Tourneur's Vindice for instance, in *The Revenger's Tragedy*, wants to avenge the murder of his fiancée; but becomes sidetracked, through his disguise as a pimp, into discovering whether he can prostitute his own sister (he can't), and then whether he can persuade his mother to act as a procuress (he can!). The knowledge he gains seems more exhilarating to him than disturbing. Likewise, with a mood of bizarre hilarity, Flamineo in Webster's *The White Devil* seeks to discover whether he can, without either provocation or conscience, murder his own brother (he can), and whether he can then watch his mother go mad without a qualm (he can't).

These are extreme enquiries, by any standard, but what marks all of them is the objectivity of the test-situations they devise. In the Chapman comedy *The Widow's Tears*, a combination of one story from Ovid and another from Petronius produces the following test: a husband wishes to discover if his wife is as true-hearted as he has always thought. He leaves on a journey, sends word home that he is dead and actually has a coffin sent back to 'prove' it. As his wife mourns in his tomb, threatening to starve herself to death, he returns in disguise as a penniless graveyard guard, and tries to seduce her over the coffin. He succeeds, and even when he tells her that he killed her husband, she proclaims, 'yet I must love thee'. Curiosity is his motive, and an objective test is his method, even though, as may be imagined, his *mood* is far from clinical. Most Jacobean experimenters are excited by what they find about human nature, no matter how appalling.

It is interesting that Shakespeare's play, though set in Vienna, has Italian names (or Roman ones). It almost seems as if Shakespeare thought that Vienna *was* in Italy, like these other plays of moral experiment; or perhaps like the immediate predecessor of Shakespeare's *Measure for Measure* in terms of a 'disguised Duke' play, John Marston's *The Malcontent*, which itself contains 'experimental' ingredients.

Marston's play features a deposed Duke, a former scholar, but now disguised as a 'malcontent' or cynic, who devotes all his energy to regaining power. He not only needs unscrupulous political skill, but comes to enjoy exercising it, becoming basically indistinguishable from and morally compromised by his role. He even experimentally tries a chastity-test. His ends are legitimate, but his means are suspect and his tactics have been aptly described as 'virtuous Machiavellianism'.

Shakespeare's similar play also features a Duke whose ends are legitimate; and, if we agree that Vincentio's motives include the strengthening of his own political power, are not too remote from those of Marston's Duke Altofronto. Part of Shakespeare's interest in the dramatic type of the Italianate disguised Duke might therefore be, on the precedent of Marston's play, to explore the use of dubious means in the pursuit of virtuous ends.

Once again, we might find ourselves questioning the morality of Vincentio's 'salvation' of his people.

This motif of moral experiment is entirely new. Before the new reign, there was no drama of moral experiment. Suddenly, there is a spate of such plays, most densely grouped around the very first Jacobean years (though also extending long afterwards in isolated plays). *Measure for Measure* exactly fits into the new pattern. It fits chronologically, actually being composed in the first year of James's reign; and it certainly fits in with the motif of experimentation with apparent innocence, complete with a clinical test-situation. Admittedly, Shakespeare's Duke is far removed from the moral nihilism of Vindice or Flamineo. He does not even have the personal interest of Chapman's husband. Yet, this makes his experiment seem all the more 'scientific'. He has no personal involvement with any of those he experiments on, and therefore his curiosity is all the purer. Certainly, however 'good' a Duke he may claim to be, his goodness consists mostly in his final rescue-operation. Otherwise, he is just as much interested as Vindice, Flamineo or Chapman's husband in finding out if apparent innocence can be corrupted. Like them, too, he successfully proves that it can be. Shakespeare is normally more associated with moral conservatism than with moral subversiveness, but this one play seems very much the product of its times. Only in the coolness with which Shakespeare treats his main character can we detect any reservations about the impulse of moral experiment to which the play is so clearly committed.

The Scholar/Duke's 'sabbatical leave'

In Webster's *Duchess of Malfi*, another play of moral enquiry, the character Bosola is the experimenter, and he is said to have stood out in his student days by his taste for arcane information. Somehow, the two things seem connected. Both are quests for obscure knowledge.

Shakespeare's Duke Vincentio is likewise an avid student, and, like so many of these plays' moral experimenters, seems essentially set apart from other men. We find this out little by little through the play. The first hint is in the first scene, where the Duke tells Angelo, whom he has just deputised, that he will 'privily' (i.e. secretly) leave the city. His explanation for this furtive departure is, 'I love the people,/ But do not like to stage me to their eyes' [67–8]. He does not condemn the idea of power as theatricality. He merely finds himself incapable of doing things that way: 'I do not relish well/ Their loud applause and *aves* vehement'. He adds that he could never trust anyone who enjoyed such things.

We have, then, even this early, the portrait of an essentially retiring man, with perhaps the hint of distaste towards his people and the idea of popularity. It is a theme which he subsequently develops in his Act I, scene iii dialogue with one Friar Thomas; a character we never again see in the play, but whose function it is to supply the Duke with a friar's habit and some instruction in how friars do things. Francis gently asks the reason for all this, and has evidently suggested, as they enter, that it has something to do with affairs of the heart. The Duke somewhat scathingly dismisses the 'dribbling dart of love' – another sure sign that he does not exactly operate as other men do – and goes on to discuss his love of 'the life removed', and his life-long deliberate avoidance of 'assemblies/ Where youth and cost a witless bravery keeps'. Vincentio is not the partying kind, and fairly explicitly despises those who are.

Later, in his disguise as Friar, pricked by Lucio's scandalous slanders about how the Duke was a 'very superficial, ignorant, unweighing fellow', he produces a self-image of considerable pomposity, as 'a scholar, a statesman, and a soldier'. A little later, again with his own reputation in mind, he complains that scandal touches even 'the whitest virtue' [III.ii.132, 137–8, 177].

The picture that very clearly emerges from all this is that the Duke dislikes the common sports and recreations of ordinary men, distrusts those who like them, personally recoils from common contact, and chooses a life of remoteness, austere 'virtue', and study.

Notably, the Duke gives no explanation of his absence to any of his political subordinates. He is 'travell'd to Poland'; that is all they know. Their assumption is that his purpose is some great affair of state. Later [IV.ii.195] when he has it rumoured that the Duke has either died, or gone into a monastery, it is readily believed. Remoteness and austerity are ingrained parts of his public image.

The neglect of the dukedom

By his own confession, the Duke's studiousness has damaged his fourteen-year reign. Specifically, it seems, his dukedom's sex-laws have gone unenforced. He speaks to Friar Thomas of his failure to enforce these 'most biting laws', and while not actually specifying the neglected statutes as sex-laws here, his simile of the 'needful bits and curbs to headstrong jades' ('jades' is a better reading than the Penguin edition's 'weeds') seems to imply that the kind of crimes involved are those of youth and wilfulness rather than viciousness. Likewise, the mention in the same speech [I.iii.19–30] of 'liberty pluck[ing] justice by the nose' seems to indicate nothing more than sins of libertinism or impudence.

His attitude to these laws and his subjects now that he feels it is time for sterner measures is intriguingly revealed in this same speech's metaphors. He speaks of the birch standing unused in the corner or of the baby beating the nurse; he compares the law to an 'o'ergrown lion in a cave,/ That goes not out to prey'. As to the first two analogies, the idea of subjects as the 'children' of their ruler is a commonplace of paternalistic government, but Vincentio's 'baby' analogy implies a more-than-usually patronising or belittling attitude in the ruler. As to the overgrown lion simile, it seems to imply that the law is a predator rather than a force of discipline.

Both of these attitudes would be consistent with a man who is about to embark on an experiment. His disrespect for his people is at least the equal of what he believes to be their disrespect for his laws. He will accordingly unleash the lion, and see the birch used on his errant children.

Vincentio's experiment

His motive for suddenly enforcing the laws could be that he has finally decided that something drastic needs to be done for his subjects' good. Also, we might take at its face value his explanation that his motive for nominating Angelo to act for him is the scruple that a Duke could not punish offences that he had so long winked at.

What makes his decision evidently experimental, rather than

judicial, however, is his decision to observe the results, and, above all, his knowledge that the substitute he appoints is suspect. He goes on to explain to Friar Thomas that, 'to behold his sway', he will, in disguise, with his own reputation 'never in the sight', 'visit both prince and people'.

Disguise is the very stock-in-trade of Shakespearean comedy. Yet, the use of disguise as a means to observe others is actually not typical. Disguise is usually donned only for survival (even if it sometimes gives incidental chances to observe others). What is more, the disguise as a friar is unique to this Shakespeare play; and when this specific disguise is used in the plays of Shakespeare's contemporaries, as Rosalind Miles reminds us (1976), it carries with it an invariably strong comic and contemptuous overtone, and implies the meddlesome and prurient nature of the disguiser.

Certainly, in adopting a disguise whose predominant function is to observe people in a specific situation, Shakespeare is very close to the husband in Chapman's comedy who wants to observe the sincerity of his wife's mourning. In both cases the act of observation is based on the conviction that all is not as it seems. Just as Chapman's husband basically already doubts his wife and sets out to test her, so the Duke here also has his doubts: specifically about the integrity of the substitute he appoints. What follows is a test of that deputy as much as anything else, and the Duke in his disguise will have the opportunity to observe scientifically the results of his experiment.

What makes this obvious are his final words to Friar Thomas concerning Angelo. These words are conspicuously sceptical of Angelo's fitness for the task ahead.

> More reasons for this action
> At our more leisure shall I render you;
> Only this one – Lord Angelo is precise,
> Stands at a guard with envy, scarce confesses
> That his blood flows, or that his appetite
> Is more to bread than stone. Hence shall we see,
> If power change purpose, what our seemers be.

This description of the deputy he has just appointed is scarcely less scathing than the scandal-mongering Lucio's accounts of him as 'a man whose blood is very snow-broth' [I.iv.57–8], and who, 'when he makes water his urine is congealed ice' [III.ii.104]. In fact, the Duke's account may be even more sceptical than Lucio's. Lucio at least seems to believe in Angelo's natural icy purity. The Duke seems rather to imply, in his statement that Angelo 'scarce *confesses* that his blood flows', or his description of him as a 'seemer', that he is at best repressed, at worst a hypocrite, and that his appetites are indeed as strong as other men's. When he goes on to speak of seeing if power will change purpose, he is directly speaking of an experiment on Angelo. Having placed this suspect character in a position of influence, he will test the proposition that all authority corrupts.

As many commentators have pointed out, it later emerges that the Duke has specific reason to doubt Angelo's virtue. He does not speak of it until Act III, but it seems that Angelo has repudiated and disgraced his former fiancée Mariana. He tells this to Isabella, and her responses – 'can this be? Did Angelo leave her so?'; and, 'what corruption in this life that it will let this man live!' – are our guide to the atrocity of his desertion. She sees Mariana's disgrace as so marked that it would be a mercy to 'take this poor maid from the world'. As already noticed in Part One ('Angelo'), hurting her feelings was not the major crime here. The real offence was the slanders which Angelo spread against her, to excuse his desertion; slanders which ruined her reputation and which rendered her unmarriageable.

We need here to put two and two together. The Duke tells Friar Peter that it will be worth watching Angelo, the 'seemer' [I.iii.end], but we later find him telling Isabella that he already knows Angelo to be no more than 'well-seeming' [III.i.224]. We are forced to acknowledge, therefore, that, in trusting power to him, he was licensing a man of known ruthlessness and inhumanity.

He also gives to that man a virtually limitless power. In fact, he gives him the impression that he has power without responsibility. His commission to Angelo is deliberately vague. In the first scene, most of his briefing of his deputy is designed to overcome Angelo's modest scruples about his unworthiness for office. He speaks of Angelo's abilities being a kind of public property, and of Nature's demand that the gift of talent be repaid by its being used. As to the nature of Angelo's responsibilities, he says only, 'In our remove be thou at full ourself./ Mortality and mercy in Vienna/ Live in thy tongue and heart' [I.i.43–5]. Later he tells him, 'Your scope is as mine own,/ So to enforce or qualify the laws/ As to your soul seems good' [64–6]. This is total power; the power of life and death. But much more telling here is the second part of the offer. Angelo's power will not even be limited by the laws of the land. By telling him that he can 'enforce or qualify' the law at will, the Duke is telling him not just that he can choose whether or not to enforce a law, but that he can nominate what he wishes the law to mean, at will. Angelo will *be* the law. The Duke also goes out of his way to remind Angelo that all this power is not to be shared. Escalus is there only as a subordinate, 'thy secondary' [46]. Notably, he gives him no specific instruction that he must enforce the sex-laws. Angelo must himself choose 'mercy' or 'mortality'.

Understandably, Angelo is rather nervous about this commission. After the Duke's exit, he and Escalus are left wondering exactly what it is that they are supposed to do. Escalus says, 'A power I have, but of what strength and nature/ I am not yet instructed', and Angelo agrees: ' 'Tis so with me' [78–81]. However, the vagueness of their assignment seems deliberate, not accidental. The Duke has no intention of giving Angelo a sense of stable bearings. He wants to let him loose with no restrictions but his own resources. And, clearly, the Duke then expects that this power will corrupt him. This is the experiment, and the stakes are high, since the entire dukedom is left at Angelo's mercy. C. Lewis (1983), whose work is basically sympathetic to the Duke, remarks all the same on the high level of risk in trusting a seedy city to a suspect man. All one can say is that the Duke's scathing remarks about common sinners indicate that his 'love' for the people [I.i.67] is more theoretical than real. His willingness to risk them to Angelo's mercies is therefore unhampered by any great gushings of tender feelings for them. The Duke who many times displays a great fondness for ingenious multi-purpose schemes, has here found a perfect one. He can move against the sexual vices that he loathes, do so without losing popularity, and at the same time test his hypothesis that his deputy is not as virtuous as he pretends. He can even observe how his people are taking all this, so that he can protect his own reputation if necessary. He settles down, in his disguise of Friar, to watch what happens.

The experiment 'takes'

Drama can be just as free with time as the novel, and the transition between the first and second scenes makes clear that Angelo's doubts and scruples are shortlived. Time is here so compressed that Angelo has hardly spoken of the uncertainty he feels, and left, than we hear of his first victim. It is the procuress Mistress Overdone who speaks of the specific arrest of Claudio for getting Juliet pregnant, and of the general proclamation about the demolition of brothels. Soon afterwards, we see Claudio being led off to prison. Part of his response is self-condemnation, as we see in his self-description as a rat which has gulped down poison. Yet, he seems reluctant to concede that what he has done is merely 'lechery', and he embarks on a description of Angelo's new measures which is notable for its rational and balanced sense of injustice. What he implies is that Angelo is a new broom, with a little too much enthusiasm for sweeping clean. The reason, Claudio thinks, might be 'the fault and glimpse of newness' (the sheer novelty of power), or that Angelo, newly in the saddle of office, wants to let the horse 'straight feel the spur' (the need to show who's boss), or possibly 'for a name' (to enhance his reputation). Either way, Angelo has immediately, and completely on his own initiative, revived all the mouldy laws, so long neglected, and Claudio is the one chosen as an example.

It is interesting that, at least at this stage, the Duke shows no signs of disquiet at the direction the experiment is taking. If he gave no direct instruction to Angelo to enforce the old laws, it is clearly his expectation and even his hope that he will do so. It was partly for this purpose that he 'on Angelo imposed the office' of deputy [I.iii.43]. He spends considerable time convincing Claudio and Juliet that their punishment is just, and by Act III claims to Escalus that he has brought Claudio to a state of mind where he accepts that he 'received no sinister measure from his judge, but most willingly humbles himself to the determination of justice' [III.ii.232]. Repeatedly, he defends Angelo's severity to others: to Lucio – 'He does well in't' [III.ii.92] – or to the Provost – 'His life is paralleled/ Even with the stroke and line of his great justice' [IV.ii.76–7].

In this, he is entirely alone. All others, from Lucio, incredulously wondering that a life should be lost 'for a game of tick-tack'

[I.ii.189]; through Escalus, gently trying to persuade Angelo to only 'cut a little' [II.i.5]; or an anonymous Justice complaining that 'Lord Angelo is severe' [II.i.269]; or the Provost exclaiming, 'it is a bitter deputy' [IV.ii.74]; or Isabella's impassioned outburst about 'man, proud man,/ Dressed in a little brief authority' [II.ii.117–18]; all other characters sound a refrain about Angelo's harshness.

But then, as we have already seen, the Duke is a character who has no more patience with common frailty than Angelo himself. In two parallel scenes involving the Duke, Angelo, and some low-life characters, it becomes clear in fact how close the Duke is to his appointed deputy in despising vice and recoiling from public contact. Angelo's is the first of these, in Act II, scene i, which begins with him rather abruptly reaffirming the order for Claudio's rapid death – 'See that Claudio/ Be executed by tomorrow morning'. More mundane judicial matters now come to his notice, to whit, an obscure complaint by the incompetent constable Elbow about the foolish Froth and the pimp Pompey. The obscurity of the case is compounded by Elbow's malapropisms – he doesn't know a malefactor from a benefactor – and the addiction to circumstantial detail of all witnesses, who seem to a man determined to discuss stewed prunes and when Froth's father died, rather than the point of the case. Even Escalus sees this as 'tedious', but Angelo rapidly runs out of all patience. Stalking off, he leaves the case to Escalus, 'Hoping that you'll find good cause to whip them all' [131]. Yet people like Elbow and Pompey are the very daily stuff of the law, and to get to the bottom of such tangled cases is the essence of judicial office.

Angelo's testy severity is exactly paralleled in the Duke's own later explosion when Elbow and Pompey encounter him. There is exactly the same intolerance – 'O heavens, what stuff is here?' [III.ii.4] – and exactly the same severity and revulsion – 'a bawd, a wicked bawd . . . a filthy vice. . . . Correction and instruction must both work/ Ere this rude beast will profit' [18, 21, 30–31].

Far from being dismayed by Angelo's severity, the Duke and he seem to see eye to eye on 'sin'. Vincentio's attitude seems little different even from Angelo's severe judgement of the meek Juliet as 'the fornicatress' [II.ii.23] or his inclusion of Claudio's affair with Juliet among 'these filthy vices' [II.iv.42].

Observing the experiment

This seems notably true of his interview with Juliet in his disguise as Friar. This is the Duke's first foray in disguise. The scene is short: a brief intermission between the two major scenes involving Angelo and Isabella. He chooses for this first excursion to visit the prison, and speak with the victims of the laws which are now being enforced. The first results are gratifying. The woman whom Angelo called 'the fornicatress' proves meekly and suitably penitent for her 'sins'. It is exactly this that the Duke is eager to find out, as his first question, 'Repent you, fair one, of the sin you carry?', reveals. He proceeds to 'try' her penitence, 'if it be sound,/ Or hollowly put on'. This at least is the only decent explanation of what he tells her, when she reveals that the 'offenceful act' was 'mutually committed': 'Then was your sin of heavier kind than his'. The idea, admittedly common in Shakespeare's time (see Part One: Text and Context: 'Chastity'), that women by their wiles and their treacherous beauty betray good men, shows the Duke's tendency, like Angelo's, to blame 'fornication' on the female.

Juliet meekly accepts the description, but even this does not satisfy the Duke. He must insist that she should be *really* sorry, not just for being punished, but for being evil. Almost impatiently, she interrupts his inquisition: 'I do repent me as it is an evil,/ And do take the shame with joy'. Her reward is to be baldly told, 'Your partner, as I hear, must die tomorrow'.

It is difficult to enjoy the Duke's behaviour in this scene. If his concern is indeed with the souls of the sinners, as if he were a real Friar, his spiritual comfort seems remarkably brusque, once he has obtained his required response. More likely, he is busily inspecting the first fruits of the new laws. Angelo has done the expected thing and enforced them. The Duke is curious to find out how his people are taking them. What better place to check for signs of mutiny than with the victims themselves? When the first of these proves pleasingly submissive and sorry for her sins, his interest in her is ended, as his callous final remark shows.

His next task is to check with the main sufferer, Claudio (Juliet's pregnancy protected her from hanging, but Claudio was less fortunate). Two scenes later, therefore, the Duke is in Claudio's cell, giving him the long and famous sermon, 'be absolute for death'. Critics too numerous to mention have found this speech overly negative; full of the horrors of life, but devoid of the merest mention of the prospect of salvation. As, therefore, a sermon preparing Claudio for death, it is so deficient that it leaves him totally open to the faint prospect of life that Isabella in a few moments offers. Having no comforting vision of a heavenly existence to come, he all-too-keenly hangs on to the existence he already has.

Of course, the Duke has no knowledge of what has developed between Angelo and Isabella. If that had not happened, the Duke's sermon would have worked well enough for his own purposes; namely to make sure that this other sexual sinner, too, was suitably cowed. The exercise must have had great piquancy for him. He had told Friar Peter that he could not directly enforce the sex-laws himself. By neglecting them, he had in a sense encouraged the vice; and he could not punish people for what he had encouraged them to do. Yet nonetheless he had placed in power a deputy whom he expected and hoped would do the job for him, and this deputy had indeed acted as planned. Therefore, if by neglecting the law the Duke had encouraged Claudio to sin, by appointing Angelo he had equally clearly acted to take Claudio's life – not personally, but at least in the general purge.

The Duke was therefore preaching to a man he had encouraged to sin, and had indirectly sentenced to death for that sin, and was telling him that he shouldn't mind dying.

Perhaps the issue then is less here Claudio's conscience than the Duke's own. No doubt the Duke would feel considerable reassurance in making Claudio meekly submit to the sentence, and could persuade himself that really all was for the best. So far, he could believe, the experiment was going exceptionally well.

Yet, he must make sure. When Claudio is immediately visited by Isabella his sister, the Duke asks the Provost to put him in a convenient listening-place.

Thence hearing that Isabella's half-offered, half-withheld offer of life has aroused Claudio's hope, and seeing Isabella's fury at him, the Duke bustles forward to calm everything down again. Lying to Claudio, he tells him that Isabella did not realise that she was only being tested by Angelo. There *was* no offer for Claudio's life. Claudio should once again resign himself to death: 'Tomorrow you must die. Go on your knees and make ready.' Claudio's request that he wants to tell Isabella that he is sorry is ignored. That is not to the Duke's purpose.

The next step is to tackle Isabella about this most stimulating development. If we remember that it was directly part of the Duke's purpose to test Angelo's 'seeming' virtue, we shall realise that the news Isabella has disclosed of Angelo's fall must be highly interesting to him: not to mention amusing. When Isabella exclaims, 'But O, how much is the good Duke deceived in Angelo! If ever he return and I can speak to him, I will ope my lips in vain, or discover his government' [III.i.193–6], the irony is of course that she is already speaking to the Duke and disclosing Angelo's government; but also that the Duke was not deceived in Angelo in the least. He already strongly suspected the man. The disclosure he has just heard confirms his best guess.

The initial experiment is now over. The Duke has discovered what he imagined he would discover: that a priggish but also suspect man placed in a position of absolute power would be corrupted by it. Of course, with Angelo's downfall, the puritanical sex-laws' reign also comes to an end. Though the Duke basically had approved of their enforcement so long as Angelo remained uncorrupted, he must now avert their effects.

The motives for experiment

It must be confessed that, so far, this has been something of an exercise in futility. That Angelo would fail was certain. All that the experiment achieved was to discover exactly what his weak spot was. The laws had been enforced, but only briefly; and now would probably have to be revoked. There seems little knowledge gained here, unless of course, by appointing a second self, the Duke wanted to discover things about himself through Angelo (see 'The Duke's self-image', below).

This in itself still seems an inadequate explanation, in the light of the Duke's behaviour when Angelo duly falls. Had he only wanted a little vicarious experience, the obvious course now would be immediately to intervene. The simplest way to do so would of course be to emerge from his disguise, confront Angelo, and punish him.

That he chooses not to do so signals his wish above all for power. Predicting men's behaviour and experimenting with it is power. Punishment is also power. But Vincentio wants more. He wants to reconstitute his own authority, and his whole relationship to his subjects. He now sees himself as a kind of carpenter of human lives, as he announces to Isabella his plan to substitute Mariana for Isabella in Angelo's bed: 'The maid will I frame and make fit for his attempt' [III.i.255–6]. A great deal of his subsequent energy is devoted to reducing the principal figures to a manageable pattern, neutralising the violent chemistry the experiment had released, and making his subjects move only according to the complex master-plans he now designs; the kind of plot which will, as he urges Isabella, 'uprighteously do a poor wronged lady a merited benefit, redeem your brother from the angry law, do no stain to your own gracious person, and much please the absent Duke' [III.i.201–5]. The ends once more are virtuous, but the motives are self-aggrandising.

The techniques of power

Notably, some of the ablest recent work on the Elizabethan and Jacobean periods has centred on the sophisticated techniques of power employed by the two sovereigns. Outstanding here is Stephen Greenblatt's work on 'Improvisation and Power' (1978).

It is Greenblatt's theory that the principal means by which the most able Europeans gained power both in their own cultures and within the newly-discovered lands was by a kind of empathy: an imaginative insinuation of themselves into the culture which was to be penetrated, followed by its conquest. The invaded culture was 'understood', but only so that it could be subverted. As examples of this gift operating within the home culture, Greenblatt quotes Elizabeth's ability to assimilate some of the power of Roman Catholicism through mimicking its church ritual; or Sir Thomas More's propaganda victory over Tyndale, through subversive imitation of his rhetoric.

Similarly, Jonathan Goldberg writes about James I's 'theatricalisation of power': his capacity, in other words, to create out of his subjects an applauding audience. Goldberg specifically refers to the public execution of criminals here. He also argues that part of James's power-play rested on his calculated annexation of the idea of family. James claimed power as the father of his people. By imitating and insinuating himself into the position of head of the house, James could draw on the instinctive ties of blood to support his claim to absolute obedience.

This material is of the highest importance to our understanding of the Duke's motivations. If we accept the presence of such persuasive ideas within the play, it may be that the Christian material is to the Duke what Catholic ritual was to Elizabeth; or that the manipulation of family is to the Duke what it was to King James.

Of course, one of the major methods of enhancing power would be to emerge as a kind of god-like figure; and so, the rescue of Claudio, the salvation of Isabella, and the ethic of mercy and forgiveness would be very serviceable to the Duke's prestige. Emerging as the sole bringer of mercy to an oppressed people, he will indeed seem, as Angelo describes him, as a 'power divine'. His power will be infinitely enhanced. Yet, what this means is that religion is assimilated into the concerns of power. The Duke's final solution still seems ethically and aesthetically pleasing, but his own motives for producing it are wholly pragmatic.

Likewise, when he takes it upon him to involve Mariana in the scheme and subdue Angelo by means of marriage (a technique he also uses on Lucio); and when he himself decides to marry Isabella; he is, by his implicit claim to dictate these marriages, also claiming a patriarchal authority over those he rules, gathering them into his fatherly power.

This is in fact the argument of Hans Sachs, who contends that Angelo is not only countered but crushed, with even his marriage-choice being denied him, as if he were a minor in his father's care. Likewise, Marcia Riefer argues that the Duke's marriage to Isabella is an act of political dominance. So powerful is the image of patriarch here, in fact, that some have seen it as almost incestuous when he proposes to the woman he has called, 'daughter'.

By and large, though, seen as power-play, the Duke's subsequent actions may now seem much less disturbing. If his motives were truly spiritual, then his manoeuvres over the last three Acts would seem sordid. If his motives are for power, we expect such things, and of course get them.

The techniques of power now exercised for the remainder of the play include a systematic, often even physical manoeuvring of his subjects' bodies, minds, and actions; deception; and a blockbusting public finale.

As to the first, in executing the 'bed-trick' he seems almost unbearably complacent as he anticipates every move.

At Mariana's house [IV.i], he enquires if he's been asked for, knowing that Isabella is due to arrive, as indeed she immediately does. In the prison [IV.ii], he asks the Provost if any messenger has yet arrived, knowing that Angelo is due to send Claudio's pardon. Again, the Penguin's Folio reading of the text slightly obscures a point: in the better editions, it is the Duke, not the Provost, who smugly announces, on the arrival of the messenger, 'And here comes Claudio's pardon' [99].

He is somewhat less smug when the messenger announces that actually, rather than being cancelled, Claudio's execution is to be speeded up. The Duke must rapidly improvise. The messenger had mentioned the execution also of one Barnadine. Vincentio hastily questions the Provost to find out what kind of offender he is: in other words, to find out if he's dispensable. He then proposes a 'head-trick' to match his earlier 'bed-trick'. Terry Eagleton comments (1986) that in *Measure for Measure* there is 'a ceaseless exchange and circulation of bodies: Angelo's for the Duke's, Isabella's (so Angelo hopes) for Claudio's, Barnadine's for Claudio's, Mariana's for Isabella's'. The point is well taken, and the inference is surely that the exchanger sees little distinction between the people he exchanges. Notably, of the four exchanges mentioned by Eagleton, three are organised by the Duke, and some sort of fourth is anticipated by him. All this is highly consistent with a man who treats his subjects as pawns.

An essential part of his plans for Acts IV and V is obfuscation. The Duke's plans are so private to himself that he confides them to nobody and indeed frequently deliberately misleads others. His plan to shorten Barnadine's life and substitute him for Claudio necessitates letting the Provost in on the bare minimum of knowledge. This is against the Duke's will – 'I will go further than I meant' – since his whole instinct is for secrecy, for keeping others in the dark; 'to veil full purpose', as he tells Isabella [IV.vi.4]. They are, after all, not people, but ciphers, pieces in his game, to move around at will.

When absolutely compelled to do so, he will use small crumbs of information: producing, for instance the Duke's own seal, to push the Provost into collaborating with the new scheme. He sees that the Provost is 'yet . . . amazed', but insists, 'this shall absolutely resolve you. Come away'. Forced finally to confide in the Provost, what the Duke then does is to provide him with a full script, which makes all the Provost's subsequent actions, notably in Act V, an exact expression of the Duke's will. When the Provost describes himself as the Duke's 'free dependent', the description is true in the sense that he is a blameless instrument, but his 'freedom' of will has by then been entirely lost.

With Isabella and Mariana he is determined to preserve their complete ignorance of his plans for them. There is clear warrant for this, since Isabella's forgiveness of Angelo can only be meaningful if she does not know of her brother's survival. However, the medicine is undeniably harsh, since by Act V he is forcing Isabella to lie, and particularly to pretend to have been defiled by Angelo, which violates all her virtuous instincts: 'To speak so indirectly I am loath./ I would say the truth' [IV.vi.1–2]. Yet the Duke's increasing possession of the lives of his subjects essentially involves the subduing or even mutation of their natures. When Isabella hears the (false) news of Claudio's death, she breaks into outraged clamour: 'Unhappy Claudio! Wretched Isabel!/ Injurious world! Most damned Angelo' [IV.iii.120–21]. Yet immediately the Duke 'tames' her, suppressing her natural feelings and channelling her into one more cure-all plot which will let her 'have your bosom on this wretch/ Grace of the Duke, revenges to your heart,/ And general honour'. Incidentally this involves another lie, the promise of revenge. The Duke has other plans here. However, the promise immediately subdues her: 'I am directed by you.'

So far, the Duke has worked in secret. Act V is different. It is a large ostentatious scene, in contrast with the intense small private scenes of the bulk of the play; and this is very striking in a Duke who claimed so clearly at the beginning to hate the '*aves* vehement' of popular acclaim. Here, though, the revival of his power demands a massive public display. And to ensure that he alone seems to hold truth and power in his hand, he produces a dénouement of extraordinary deceptiveness and complexity, all scripted. The ladies tell their prepared story, with Isabella lying that she lay with Angelo; another of the Duke's hacks, Friar Peter discredits Isabella, as planned; the Duke briefly exits, re-enters as the Friar, then stuns his subjects by proving to be the Duke; he exposes, marries off, and judges Angelo; and so becomes the figure of godlike power whom all plead to for mercy.

Isabella's lie ensures that Angelo still thinks he controls

the truth. With Friar Peter's denunciation and the Duke's encouragement to him to punish Isabella and Mariana to his 'height of pleasure', Angelo is sure he is safe. He can then be all the more heavily crushed when the truth emerges. With Isabella already tamed, the Duke can use the exaggerated device of marrying Angelo to Isabella's friend Mariana, and then threatening to make Mariana a widow, to change Isabella from a vocal avenger into a meek suppliant. She 'chooses' mercy, but is manoeuvred into doing so.

By these extraordinary devices, by lies, by deliberate public exposure, the Duke insinuates himself deep into his subjects' private lives so as to control them; and by skilfully mimicking the processes of Christian redemption he plays God at his subjects' expense.

The obstructions to control

Control does not at all times come easily to the Duke. Angelo's treacherous decision to sleep with Isabella (as he thinks) and also execute her brother clearly catches Vincentio off guard; though it must be said that on this occasion he improvises with exceptional skill and speed. Elsewhere, the ragged edges begin to show. There is a distinct impression of haste as he summons up his cohorts: 'Go call Flavius' house,/ And tell him where I stay. Give the like notice/ To Valentius, Rowland, and to Crassus,/ And bid them bring the trumpets to the gate;/ But send me Flavius first.' Certainly there is no time for the elaborate welcome pageant found in Whetstone's play, the main source. When Angelo reads Vincentio's scrambled letters announcing his return, he says they 'show much like to madness' [IV.iv.4].

Worst of all, though, are the occasions when the Duke's will is directly opposed. Such is the force of his drive towards absolute control that he seems most disturbed when his plans are resisted by others. Take for instance the case of Barnadine, where what bothers him is not Barnadine's crime but his refusal to die on cue. When it is clear that Angelo still intends to execute Claudio, the Duke's plan is of course to substitute Barnadine. Barnadine, however, rather endearingly, is belligerently drunk, and 'will not consent to die this day, that's certain' [IV.iii.53–4]. His refusal reduces the Duke to spluttering impotence – 'Unfit to live or die. O gravel heart!' – and he is about to drag Barnadine to his death – 'After him, fellows: bring him to the block' – until the Provost produces a still more convenient corpse, the pirate Ragozine, physically similar to Claudio, and dead that morning of a fever. Then his self-control resumes, as does his usual human chess-game: 'Put them in secret holds. Both Barnadine/ And Claudio' [IV.iii.85–6].

The same sort of thing very notably happens with Lucio, whose dissenting voice is hard to quell. It is not just that the descriptions of the Duke that Lucio produces are uncomfortably close to the truth: that, for instance, the description of him as 'the old fantastical Duke of dark corners' [IV.iii.155–6] so uncannily hits on the Duke's voyeurism and secrecy. In truth, any unscripted voice is unwelcome. Everything must conform to the Duke's pattern. In Act IV, scene iii the Duke seems almost prepared to flee from Lucio (who, however, is not easy to shake – 'I am a kind of burr, I shall stick'). In Act V, far more evidently, the Duke's impatience becomes almost violent. Lucio here persists in thrusting his comments into the Duke's careful scenario. Mariana describes herself as, 'neither maid, widow, nor wife': all literally true, since she is a 'wife' in fact but not yet in form. Lucio remarks that she must be a whore, then, since 'many of them are neither maid, widow, nor wife'. The comment is highly amusing, and therefore damaging to the seriousness of the Duke's scheme. His response is angry, though still ironic: 'Silence that fellow. I would he had some cause/ To prattle for himself' [181–82]. When Lucio tries another joke, the irony entirely disappears: 'Sirrah, no more' [212].

Interestingly, he uses with Lucio the same pattern of deception and revelation that he has so far used with all the others. By the end of Act V, he has threatened Isabella and Mariana with pun-ishment to the 'height of [Angelo's] pleasure'; he has continued the pretence that Claudio is dead; he has sworn to execute Angelo after having him formally but forcibly married to Mariana; he has pretended to continue to insist on that execution, even after Isabella's heartfelt plea for mercy; and he has threatened to dismiss the Provost. All therefore at the end seem under threat – of death, of widowhood, of dismissal, of having lost a brother. Then, miraculously, at the end, the Duke can produce life out of death: a living brother, and therefore a living Angelo (provided that the sex-laws are no longer enforced). All at the end of the play owe the Duke their lives, their happiness, their future. It is in this context that he can offer his hand in marriage to a nun and expect her to accept it gratefully.

He uses precisely the same formula with Lucio. He insists that he will marry him to the whore he had made pregnant; and that then he will be whipped and hanged. The last two punishments are then commuted. 'Thy slanders I forgive', the Duke says. Lucio must only marry the whore.

The Duke's self-image

Yet Lucio continues to object. He does not want to marry the whore. It is worse than whipping and hanging. The Duke's reply is revealing: 'slandering a prince deserves it'. In other words, Lucio's slanders are not in fact forgiven: his marriage to the whore is his punishment. Lucio had struck the Duke on his most delicate point, his self-image.

In fact, this self-image is extraordinarily sensitive. We have seen already how Lucio's slanders about the Duke's sympathy to lechery, or his ignorance, or his secretiveness, provoke the Duke into giving a lilywhite version of himself; in his own eyes, evidently, he is 'a scholar, a statesman and a soldier' [III.ii.137–38], 'never . . . much detected for women' [116], and possessed of 'the whitest virtue' [177]. His soliloquy at the end of the scene is in much the same vein, and countless critics have commented on the extraordinary stiffness of its verse, reinforcing the sense of a rigid rectitude in the attitude of the speech. Clearly, Vincentio thinks of himself as a paragon of leaders:

> He who the sword of heaven will bear
> Should be as holy as severe;
> Pattern in himself to know,
> Grace to stand and virtue go;
> More nor less to others paying
> Than by self-offences weighing.

He goes on to contrast and criticise the hypocrisy of Angelo.

Yet clearly this confident self-image is far from secure. Just a few words earlier, he had been asking Esacalus – in his disguise of Friar, of course – 'Of what disposition was the Duke?' He needs to know what others think of him, especially in the light of Lucio's remarks. No doubt he was gratified by Escalus' response. His faithful old subordinate has thoroughly bought the official version, and describes the Duke as one 'that, above all other strifes, contended especially to know himself' [220–22].

This is intriguingly both true and untrue. Insofar as the Duke persists in idealising himself, he is in error. Yet, his experiment on Angelo reveals an intriguing drive to find out about himself. This Duke has no relatives nor enemies in the play, and in this sense no personal motive for what he does. Yet it is a second self that he places in power, and licenses, as he could never license himself. This is what Jonathan Goldberg may mean in his intriguing comment that 'the Duke authorises and authors' Angelo's actions (1983). He can enjoy the effects of severity in his celibate disguise, seeing how the victims take their punishment. And when Angelo (who, like the Duke, fancies he is immune from the 'dribbling dart of love') actually falls victim to passion, the Duke can assert his own distance from such disgraceful things.

Yet the Duke's marriage proposals to Isabella show his actual near-identity with Angelo's sexuality as well as with his loathing of sex. After Act III, therefore, he seeks a legitimate outlet for the desires he has revealed in and through his surrogate. Framing others to respectable forms, creating only predicted responses, substituting identities of the Duke's choice for the identities people actually possess, he is able also to reorder his own life. Certainly, the Duke is the chief beneficiary of the play. He has come to terms with sex, and he possesses Isabella, the woman who has a clear sex-appeal to puritans. As it happens, this is all very much at Angelo's expense. In his life as a private citizen he had been respected and self-respecting. Given power, brought face to face with his own violent sexuality and treachery, and then publicly humiliated, everything he valued is destroyed by the end of the play. He has his life, but we cannot imagine he believes it worth living.

For the Duke, however, he has been most useful, taking the risks and making the appalling disclosures which the Duke dared not make, on the Duke's behalf. The experiment is indeed an extraordinary attempt by the Duke to know himself, and the true concealed subject of that experiment is himself.

Yet the Duke is unaware of this. Up to the end of the play, he maintains a self-image of uncomplicated self-righteousness.

Take for instance his comments while still disguised as a Friar: 'I have seen corruption boil and bubble/ Till it o'errun the stew' [V.i.316–17]. The pun on 'stew' (= brothel) once again shows that when he thinks of sin he thinks only of sex, and the indignation is clearly not feigned, but his own real feelings.

Yet, of course, his strict morality is far from consistent. To be explicit, his values are at the service of his political skills, if need be. A good example are his words (aside) when Angelo's man brings, as Vincentio believes, Claudio's pardon. They reveal anything but 'liberal' values: 'This is his pardon, purchased by such sin/ For which the pardoner himself is in'. This indicates that, as far as the Duke is concerned, both Angelo and Mariana are sinners: the pardoner who now releases Claudio, and the one who purchased it with her body (on the Duke's own advice). When therefore he had assured Mariana, 'To bring you thus together, 'tis no sin' [IV.i.72], he lied: a lie which looks all the more devious since he is here using the spiritual authority of his disguise as Friar to make Mariana do something which he privately believed would endanger her soul. Of course, as far as the Duke is concerned, all this is in a good cause, but it is worth pointing out that his plan actively subverts the laws which he designed should be enforced, and violates the moral code in which he believes.

So, clearly, while the Duke continues to think of himself as a righteous man, his personal values are actually at the mercy of his drive towards power. This also supersedes any abstract concern for justice, mercy, or even the law. A mob of critics have pointed out how the sex-laws are first of all neglected, then entrusted to a man likely to enforce them with the utmost severity (but also to abuse them), and finally casually dropped, leaving the 'stew' as merrily bubbling at the end as at the beginng. All this seems to compel us to see the Duke's motives in personal terms: not as one whose whole concern is the welfare of his people, spiritual or temporal, but as one who will use his power to satisfy his own ends.

Conclusion

It is easy to over-react to the Duke; easy to forget that Dukes once possessed real power, and that the duty of subjects was obedience. It is therefore important to sift out from our responses that part of us that resents the Duke, simply because he thinks he has the right to manipulate his subjects. The fact is that rulers of that time – kings in England, and sometimes Dukes abroad – *did* have that right.

Having said that, we may nevertheless still enjoy Shakespeare's detached study of the operation of power, and the moral contradictions, the manipulation of others, and the essential egotism which it involves.

At the beginning of the play, we see a Duke who has lost control as a leader. He has neglected the laws, hidden himself from his people, let slip his power. He decides by a gigantic act of will to rescue the situation. After such profound neglect, nothing but a major political ploy would restore his authority. It is too late merely to put on a show for his people. They must also become actors in the process and contributors to it. He needs to manoeuvre them into recreating him in a more loveable image. He does not of course love them. His only interest in the love between people and prince is in capitalising on it for the purposes of power.

The first ploy is indeed to nominate a substitute. This is a political risk, since the substitute might prove to be a popular ruler. Vincentio minimises the risks by appointing a man he was almost certain would fail. He stands by with a genuine scientific curiosity to see exactly how Angelo will fail. Part of his interest here is clearly personal. He is observing his second self. He also observes with equal pleasure the gratifying effects of the laws that are enforced, and the submission of the sufferers to those laws.

This is the essential first move in a double process. He creates out of Angelo an enemy of the people. The rest of his endeavour is devoted to creating a situation by which he, the Duke, can appear in a good light. As Terrell Tebbetts argues, he can interpose himself between the people and the law, and thereby become 'a kind of saviour of the people from the law'.

Everything in Act V is designed to enhance the Duke's image. He is the merciful lord, the dispenser of pardons, the miraculous resurrector of a dead man. More broadly, as with the whole of Act V, the Duke is the great discloser. He had vowed in advance, regarding Isabella and the survival of Claudio, 'I will keep her ignorant of her good,/ To make her heavenly comforts of despair/ When it is least expected' [IV.iii.107–9]. He is mightily pleased with himself in the process. This surely is the 'theatricalisation of power', as Goldberg describes it, and he places himself as the giver of things 'heavenly'.

This very broadly accounts for the difficulty that so many have with the play: that it seems to strip a tragic conflict and powerful characters of their life and autonomy in the second half; or that the characters become merely interchangeable. In truth, the 'stripping' is not Shakespeare's but the Duke's. It is he who determinedly subverts the identity of others, to reassert his own power. H.C. Cole seems very much to locate this central point when he complains that Vincentio 'usurps' the righteous forces of monarch and God, 'but taints each in the process' (1983).

Part of the purpose of both the experiment and the exercise of power is highly personal. Rosalind Miles spoke more truly than she perhaps knew in describing Angelo as 'a symbolic externalisation of the Duke'. The truest sense of this is that Angelo enacts for the watching Duke the temptations of power which he has never permitted himself. The Duke seizes – legitimately – at the end of the play the fruits of those temptations. He has, in the process, come to know himself a little. He can at least acknowledge his wish to possess Isabella, which is a great advance on his earlier contempt for the 'dribbling dart of love'. Yet, his chilly response to Lucio's unforgettable remarks about the 'old fantastical Duke of dark corners' who 'would have dark deeds darkly answered' tells us that there are truths which lie well beyond his wish for self-knowledge. Indeed, it is only the flattering glass in which he wishes to be seen: only the reflection of his own glory and power, as saviour of his people.

Yet, in Isabella's silence at the Duke's repeated marriage proposals, a silence shared by the whole of the rest of the cast at the end, we can see at the very least, that their reaction is rather stunned than ecstatic. The pleasures the Duke has enjoyed in Act V are rather too manipulative and private to be the cause of immediate general rejoicing. Shakespeare, by this, and by the intractability of Barnadine and Lucio, signifies his own withheld approval. J.W. Lever's remark is well worth repeating: 'no man's life is so worthless as to be sacrificed to another's convenience' (1965). Yet this is precisely the order of priorities which the Duke consistently proposes: literally, with Barnadine, metaphorically with all the others.

The process is most marked with Angelo. The Duke does in truth have much to thank Angelo for. Yet, at the end of this play, Shakespeare's most sophisticated exploration of the political mind, Angelo is the discarded victim of the Duke's exercise of political and sexual power.

This might, though it is stretching a point, be thought of as a 'good': for Angelo, pretentious and false (though comparatively harmless), to have been exposed from his respected position and crushed. Certainly, with Isabella, many critics have spoken of the real advances made by her during the play.

It is important, though, not to confuse good results with good intentions. The Duke, in truth, has little interest in benefiting Angelo or Isabella. For him, this is not an exercise in spiritual salvation for himself or his subjects. It is an exercise in power. All that eventually matters to him, regarding religion, is that he should *seem* to produce things holy. The Christian ethic of mercy is highly serviceable, when he is the bringer of it. Yet, it covers wholesale manipulations of people, morality, and the law. The Duke – named Vincentio only in the *dramatis personae* – has little enough of any stable trait of identity beyond his drive for power: certainly not holiness. His purposes are no more than a useful imitation of Christianity, as much of a cloak of godliness and no more profound than his disguise as a nameless friar.

References

The ten most highly recommended sources are marked *.

Brief introductory studies

* Barton, Anne, '*Measure for Measure*', in *The Riverside Shakespeare*, ed. G. Blakemore Evans et. al. (Boston, 1974), pp. 545–9.
* Lever, J.W., ed., *Measure for Measure* (London, 1965; The Arden Shakespeare Series), Introduction, pp. xi–xcviii.

Studies of the play's type (comedy, tragi-comedy, etc.) and conventions

Beckerman, Bernard, 'Shakespeare Closing', *Kenyon Review*, 7 (1985), pp. 79–95.

Bryant, J.A., Jr, *Shakespeare and the Uses of Comedy* (Lexington, Kentucky, 1986), pp. 215–20.

Edwards, Philip, *Shakespeare and the Confines of Art* (London, 1968), especially pp. 108–19.

Foakes, R.A., *Shakespeare, the Dark Comedies to the Last Plays: from Satire to Celebration* (Charlottesville, Virginia, 1971), pp. 17–31.

Frye, Northrop, *A Natural Perspective: The Development of Shakespearean Comedy and Romance* (New York, 1965), especially pp. 118–59.

Frye, Northrop, *The Myth of Deliverance: Reflections on Shakespeare's Problem Comedies* (Toronto, 1983), pp. 3–33.

Honigmann, E.A.J., '*Measure for Measure*', *Proceedings of the British Academy*, 67 (1981), pp. 101–21.

Howard, Jean E., '*Measure for Measure* and the Restraints of Convention', *Essays in Literature*, 10 (1983), pp. 149–58.

Kay, Dennis, 'To Hear the Rest Untold: Shakespeare's Postponed Endings', *Renaissance Quarterly*, 37 (1984), pp. 207–27.

Kirsch, Arthur C., 'The Integrity of *Measure for Measure*', *Shakespeare Survey*, 28 (1975), pp. 94–106.

Lascelles, Mary, *Shakespeare's 'Measure for Measure'* (London, 1953; New York, 1970).

Lawrence, W.W., *Shakespeare's Problem Comedies* (New York, 1931), pp. 78–121.

Schanzer, Ernest, *The Problem Plays of Shakespeare* (New York, 1965), pp. 71–131.

Tillyard, E.M.W., *Shakespeare's Problem Plays* (Toronto, 1951).

Sources, and parallel plots in medieval and renaissance literature

Cole, H.C., 'Shakespeare's Comedies and their Sources, some Biographical and Artistic Inferences', *Shakespeare Quarterly*, 34 (1983), pp. 405–19, especially p. 416.

Cox, J.D., 'The Medieval Background of *Measure for Measure*', *Modern Philology*, 81 (1983), pp. 1–13.

* Miles, Rosalind, *The Problem of 'Measure for Measure': A Historical Investigation* (New York, 1976).

Salingar, Leo, *Shakespeare and the Traditions of Comedy* (Cambridge, 1974), pp. 298–303, 319–25.

Spinrad, P.S., '*Measure for Measure* and the Art of Not Dying', *Texas Studies in Literature and Language*, 26 (1984), pp. 74–93.

Background of contemporary Ideas

A. ON KINGSHIP AND SPECIFIC PARALLELS BETWEEN THE DUKE AND KING JAMES I

* Bennett, Josephine Waters, *Measure for Measure as Royal Entertainment* (New York and London, 1966).

* Goldberg, Jonathan, *James I and the Politics of Literature* (Baltimore and London, 1983), especially pp. 81–6, 149, 184, 231–9.

Greenblatt, Stephen, 'Improvisation and Power', in *Literature and Society: Selected Papers from the English Institute, 1978*, ed. Edward W. Said (Baltimore, 1980), especially pp. 57–66.

Price, J.E., 'Back-Wounding Calumny: the Subject of Slander in King James' *Basilikon Doron* and Shakespeare's *Measure for Measure*', *American Notes and Queries*, 22 (1984), pp. 99–101.

Schoeck, R.J., review article, *Shakespeare Quarterly*, 31 (1980), pp. 445–9.

Tebbetts, Terrell L., 'Talking Back to the King', *College Literature*, 12 (1985), pp. 122–34.

Tennenhouse, Leonard, 'Representing Power: *Measure for Measure* in its Time', *Genre*, 15 (1982), pp. 139–56.

B.   ON CHASTITY

Bond, Ronald B., ' "Dark Deeds Darkly Answered": Thomas Becon's *Homily Against Whoredom and Adultery*, its Contexts and its Affiliations with 3 Shakespearean Plays', *Sixteenth Century Journal*, 16 (1985), pp. 191–205.

Corre, Alan D., 'The Lecher, the Coward and the Virtuous Woman', *Folklore*, 92 (1981), pp. 25–9.

Geckle, George L., 'Shakespeare's Isabella', *Shakespeare Quarterly*, 22 (1971), pp. 163–8.

Rosenheim, Judith, ' "Sounding Breaks of Ice" ', *Shakespeare Quarterly*, 35 (1984), pp. 87–91.

C.   ON MARRIAGE AND BETROTHAL LAW

Harding, D.P., 'Elizabethan Betrothals and *Measure for Measure*', *J.E.G.Ph.*, 49 (1950), pp. 140–58.

Nagarajan, S., '*Measure for Measure* and Elizabethan Betrothals', *Shakespeare Quarterly*, 14 (1963), pp. 115–19.

Nuttall, A.D., '*Measure for Measure*: the Bed-Trick', *Shakespeare Survey*, 28 (1975), pp. 51–6.

Scott, Margaret, ' "Our City's Institutions": some Further Reflections on the Marriage Contracts in *Measure for Measure*', *ELH*, 49 (1982), pp. 790–804.

Wentersdorf, Karl P., 'The Marriage Contracts in *Measure for Measure*', *Shakespeare Survey*, 32 (1979), pp. 129–44.

Themes

A.   JUSTICE AND EQUITY

Dickson, J.W., 'Renaissance Equity and *Measure for Measure*', *Shakespeare Quarterly*, 13 (1962), pp. 287–97.

Dunkel, W., 'Law and Equity in *Measure for Measure*', *Shakespeare Quarterly*, 13 (1962), pp. 275–85.

Hunter, R.G., *Shakespeare and the Comedy of Forgiveness* (New York and London, 1965).

B.   RELIGIOUS INTERPRETATIONS

Battenhouse, Roy, '*Measure for Measure* and the Christian Doctrine of the Atonement', *P.M.L.A.*, LXI (1946), pp. 1029–59.

Coghill, Nevill, 'Comic Form in *Measure for Measure*', *Shakespeare Survey*, 8 (1955), pp. 14–27.

* Gless, Darryl J., '*Measure for Measure*', the Law and the Convent (Princeton, 1979).

Knight, G. Wilson, '*Measure for Measure* and the Gospels', in *The Wheel of Fire* (London, 1930), pp. 80–106.

Leavis, F.R. '*Measure for Measure*', in *The Common Pursuit* (London, 1952), pp. 160–72.

Pope, Elizabeth M., 'The Elizabethan Background of *Measure for Measure*', *Shakespeare Survey*, 2 (1949), pp. 66–82.

Schleiner, L., 'Providential Improvisation in *Measure for Measure*', *P.M.L.A.*, 97 (1982), pp. 227–36.

Winston, Matthew, 'Morality Play Elements in *Measure for Measure*', in *Shakespeare Studies*, ed. J. Leeds Barroll III, XIV (1981), pp. 229–48.

C.   OTHER

Eagleton, Terry, *William Shakespeare* (Oxford, 1986), pp. 48–58 (on the theme of exchanges).

Ewbank, Inga-Stina, 'Shakespeare's Liars', *Proceedings of the British Academy*, 69 (1984), pp. 141–43 (on the theme of deception).

* Hawkins, Harriet, ' "The Devil's Party": Virtues and Vices in *Measure for Measure*', *Shakespeare Survey*, 31 (1978), pp. 105–13 (on the theme of interchangeable values).

Huebert, Ronald, 'Taking the Measure of Manliness', *Dalhousie Review*, 63 (1983), pp. 125–34 (on the theme of varying standards of manhood).

Leech, Clifford, 'The Meaning of *Measure for Measure*', *Shakespeare Survey*, 3 (1950), pp. 66–73 (an anti-thematic approach).

Palmer, Christopher, 'Selfness in *Measure for Measure*', *Essays in Criticism*, XXVIII (1978), pp. 187–207 (on the theme of egotism).

Feminist studies

* Jardine, Lisa, *Still Harping on Daughters: Women and Drama in the Age of Shakespeare* (Sussex, 1983), especially pp. 181–93.
Riefer, Marcia, ' "Instruments of Some Mightier Member": the Constriction of Female Power in *Measure for Measure*', *Shakespeare Quarterly*, 35 (1984), pp. 157–69.

Theatre studies

Charney, Maurice, 'Televisionary Shakespeare: Working with the Shakespeare Hour', *Shakespeare Quarterly*, 36 (1985), pp. 489–95.
Coursen, H.R., 'Why *Measure for Measure*?', *Film Quarterly*, 12 (1984), pp. 65–9.
Nicholls, Graham, *'Measure for Measure': Text & Performance* (London, 1986).
Scott, Michael, *Renaissance Drama and a Modern Audience* (London and Atlantic Highlands, 1982), pp. 61–75.
Sohlich, Wolfgang, 'Prologomenon for a Theory of Drama Reception: Peter Brook's *Measure for Measure* and the Emergent Bourgeoisie', *Comparative Drama*, 18 (1984), pp. 54–8.
Willson, Robert F., 'The BBC-TV *Measure for Measure* and Television Aesthetics, *New York Shakespeare Society Bulletin*, 4 (1986), pp. 23–5.

Psychological studies, of Shakespeare or his characters

Brown, Carolyn, 'Erotic Religious Flagellation and Shakespeare's *Measure for Measure*', *ELH*, 16 (1986), pp. 139–65.
Brown, Carolyn (b), '*Measure for Measure*: Isabella's Beating Fantasies', *American Imago*, 43 (1986), pp. 67–80.
Holbrook, David, 'The Crow of Avon: Shakespeare, Sex and Ted Hughes', *Cambridge Quarterly*, 15 (1986), pp. 1–12.
Kliman, Bernice W., 'Isabella in *Measure for Measure*', *Shakespeare Studies*, ed. J. Leeds Barroll III, XV (1982), pp. 137–48.
Sachs, Hans, 'The Measure in *Measure for Measure*', in *The Design Within*, ed. M.D. Faber (New York, 1970), pp. 479–97.
Wheeler, Richard P., *Shakespeare's Development and the Problem*

Comedies: Turn and Counter-Turn (Berkeley, 1981), pp. 5–33, 92–153.

Studies specifically of the Duke

Bawcutt, N.W., ' "He Who the Sword of Heaven Will Bear": the Duke versus Angelo in *Measure for Measure*', *Shakespeare Survey*, 37 (1984), pp. 89–97.
Hillman, R., '*The Tempest* as Romance and Anti-Romance', *University of Toronto Quarterly*, 55 (1986), p. 59, n. 18.
Kay, Dennis, ' "To Hear the Rest Untold": Shakespeare's Postponed Endings', *Renaissance Quarterly*, 37 (1984), pp. 218–19.
* Levin, R.A., 'Duke Vincentio and Angelo: "Would a Feather Turn the Scale?" ', *Studies in English Literature*, 22 (1982), pp. 257–70.
Lewis, C., ' "Dark Deeds Darkly Answered": Duke Vincentio and Judgement in *Measure for Measure*', *Shakespeare Quarterly*, 34 (1983), pp. 271–89.
Moore, S., 'Virtue and Power in *Measure for Measure*', *English Studies*, 63 (1982), pp. 308–17.

Other

Berry, Ralph, review of the New Variorum edition of *Measure for Measure*, ed. M. Eccles, *Queens Quarterly*, 88 (1981), pp. 536–43.
Stevenson, David Lloyd, *The Achievement of Shakespeare's 'Measure for Measure'* (Ithaca, 1966).
Wharton, T.F., ' "Yet I'll Venture": Moral Experiment in Jacobean Tragedy', *Salzburg Studies in English*, 95 (1980), pp. 3–17.
Wharton, T.F., *Moral Experiment in Jacobean Drama* (London, 1988).

Index